MIRACLES
OF THE
ORTHODOX
CHURCH

The Miracles of Christ Perpetuated in the Orthodox Church

MARY EFROSINI GREGORY

LIGHT & LIFE PUBLISHING COMPANY MINNEAPOLIS, MINNESOTA

Light & Life Publishing Company
P.O. Box 26421
Minneapolis, MN 55426-0421
P: (952) 925-3888
Web: www.light-n-life.com

Copyright © 2009
Mary Efrosini Gregory

Chapters 1-5 inclusive and part of Chapter 8 from *An Eastern Orthodox View of Pascal*
by Mary Efrosini Gregory. Reprinted by permission of Light & Life Publishing Company.

ISBN: 978-1-933654-24-9
Library of Congress Control Number: 2009921968

This book is dedicated to our Lord and Savior Jesus Christ in gratitude for His very generous gift of everlasting life.

PREFACE

Biblical references will be according to the
King James Version, unless otherwise indicated.

TABLE OF CONTENTS

INTRODUCTION

But you are a chosen people, a royal priesthood, a holy nation, a people belonging to God, that you may declare the praises of him who called you out of darkness into his wonderful light. Once you were not a people, but now you are the people of God; once you had not received mercy, But now you have received mercy.

—1 Pet 2:9-10 (NIV)

An examination of the miracles of the Orthodox Church reveals a significant fact: wherever and whenever the Church has been persecuted, God has poured forth miracles to His people as signs of His presence and to strengthen their faith. Politics, persecution, and miracles are intimately intertwined. This truth becomes evident when one analyzes newspaper articles of miracles that have been authenticated by the hierarchies of the Orthodox churches around the world. For example, on April 21, 1991 blood gushed forth from communion bread in an Orthodox church in Zarka, Jordan, as a sign that God was present and watching over the multitudes of Orthodox

Christians who were forced to flee Iraq and relocate to Jordan after the Gulf War. This miracle has been authenticated by Diodorus I, Patriarch of Jerusalem. Furthermore, the miracle-working, incorruptible relics of Saint Alexander of Svir have been preserved despite the aggressive campaign of the Bolshevik Revolution of 1917 to destroy all holy things. The Saint's relics were found in 1997 and they continue to perform miracles of healing to this very day, as they had done back in 1533. An outpouring of miracles occurred in 1997-1998, where his incorruptible relics were laid out, at the Faith, Hope, and Love Chapel at the Pokrovo-Tervenichi Convent, St. Petersburg, Russia. Miracles continued to be reported there, even after his remains were returned to the monastery that he had founded, the Svirsky Monastery. Saint Alexander's miracles have been authenticated by Alexey II, Patriarch of Moscow and All Russia.

Moreover, St. Nicholas Albanian Orthodox Church in Chicago has an icon of Mary holding the Infant Jesus that began to weep and perform miracles of healing intermittently in the late 1980s and throughout the 1990s. The weeping was declared to be a miraculous sign by Archbishop Iakovos of the Greek Orthodox Archdiocese of North and South America. The miraculous icon was featured on the Leeza Show. When Leeza Gibbons asked the priest of St. Nicholas Church, "Why here? Why now?" he responded that he believed that it was because a large number of people had recently arrived from the former Soviet Union and its satellite countries where they had not been free to practice their faith. The miracle occurred at a time when the church was filled with Orthodox Christians who were attending church for the first time in their lives. This outpouring of God's mercy glorified Him and constituted the exultant, triumphant celebration of the victory of good over evil, of Christianity over atheism, of religious freedom at long last after the extreme persecution of the Church, of Heaven over hell. One must necessarily extrapolate that a causality exists between the persecution of the Lord's Bride, the Orthodox Church, and the amazing outpouring of God's miracles that has received coverage, frequently on the front page, of the major newspapers of the world.

Also of great significance is the miracle of the blinking and weeping icon of Christ that faces the site of His birth in the Church of the Nativity, Bethlehem, West Bank. This miracle was authenticated by Father Anastasios, on behalf of the Greek Orthodox Patriarchate of Jerusalem. When it first happened, during the week of Oct. 27, 1996, many pilgrims to the Holy Land believed that this miracle, in which the icon of Christ shed tears of blood, announced political strife. As it turned out, that is exactly what it did. The year before it happened, in December 1995, Yasser Arafat's wife, Suha, placed her baby on the silver star marking the Lord's birthplace and she knelt before her baby in mock prayer. Her actions appeared to simulate the Nativity scene. This is sacrilege, to say the least, but this disrespect marked the onset of evil behavior that got progressively worse. After the miracle of the icon's blinking and weeping tears of blood occurred a year later, violence erupted and continued for many years. Human bloodshed gradually reached a crescendo, ending in the occupation of the Church of the Nativity for 38 days by Palestinian militants during April 2-May 10, 2002. The occupiers desecrated the church by urinating everywhere, strewing toilet paper all about, ripping up Bibles, and using the pages as toilet paper. When the Israel Defense Forces (IDF) finally removed the militants through negotiation, they found 40 explosive devices in the Church. The icon overlooking Christ's birthplace, weeping tears of blood, announced that violence was on the horizon; it reminds us that the Prince of Peace has come to earth, bringing great and wonderful gifts-eternal life, the healing of the rift between God and man, theosis, and a new identity in Him-and that tragically, he was rejected both by His own and then by the followers of Mohammed six centuries later. It reminds us that the Lord, looking into the future, once wept over Jerusalem two millennia ago (Luke 19:41-44). Associated Press Television covered the story and Chapter Eight includes dialogue taken from the transcript of APTV's online archives. Also included is material from CNN, the *Jerusalem Post*, the *Times-Picayune*, and a front page story from the *New York Times*.

The God of the Christians is a God who has historically interacted with His people and who continues to have an ongoing, eternal relationship with them. He changes lives, performs miracles, communicates with and advises His children in their hearts during prayer, and has instructed them to remain pure and holy, apart and distinct from the rest of the world. The objective of this study is to enumerate and examine miracles that the Lord has performed as signs of His love, faithfulness, compassion, mercy, presence, and watchfulness over His flock. We try to accomplish this task by addressing Christianity's great wealth of miracles in chronological order: first, the biblical period (the miracles that preceded the birth of Christ, those that were performed by Him, and those that occurred at the time of His Resurrection and Ascension into Heaven); the miracles in the Temple during the years 30 AD-70AD; miracles that have continued during the Church age (the Miracle of the Holy Flame, miracles performed by the saints, miracles on Mt. Athos); finally, miracles that occur in the news today and that have been authenticated by the hierarchy of the Orthodox Church. We have restricted the chapter on contemporary miracles to those that have been authenticated by Orthodox archdioceses for two reasons: first, it is imperative to weed out signs and wonders that are the results of demonic activity. Secondly, it is unfortunate, but history has shown that people resort to proclaiming false miracles in order to make money. By limiting our coverage to miracles that have been authenticated by patriarchs and archbishops, we ensure that we are giving the public pure flour to consume, rather than flour sifted with sand.

The first five chapters of this book contain material on miracles reprinted from my previous book, *An Eastern Orthodox View of Pascal*. That book is an examination of how the seventeenth century French philosopher, Blaise Pascal, in his classic work, *Thoughts* [*Pensées*], proves that God exists. *An Eastern Orthodox View of Pascal* addresses Pascal's use of probability theory to prove that the fulfillment of hundreds of Messianic prophecies in the person of one man, Jesus Christ, the historicity of miracles, and the unity between the OT and New (ie: textual evidence of the Holy Trinity in the OT and typology), clearly fall outside the realm of random chance and therefore, are proofs of Christ and of the existence of Divine Will. Pascal's second proof of God's existence, miracles, deserves further examination and coverage in an entirely separate book: miracles have been continuous and ongoing throughout the Church Age and the subject is vast and endless.

CHAPTER ONE ("Christ's Power to Resurrect the Dead") highlights the greatest of all of the miracles that Christ performed: He raised the dead. This is a feat that only God Himself can accomplish. Christ predicted His own resurrection and then raised Himself on Sunday morning, significantly, on the Feast of the First Fruits. Many people saw the resurrected Christ: He appeared to the women at the empty tomb, to Peter and Cleopas on the road to Emmaus, to the disciples in the Upper Room on two occasions; Thomas touched His pierced hands and put his hand in His pierced side; He appeared to the disciples in the fishing boat on the Sea of Tiberius; Paul advises that more than 500 people saw Him at one time and that many of these witnesses were still alive (implying that they were still available for interview).

In addition, He resurrected the widow's son at Nain; Jairus' 12 year old daughter; His friend, Lazarus; and after He surrendered His Ghost on the Cross, the tombs opened and the bodies of many OT saints were resurrected and were seen by many in Jerusalem (Mat 27:52). Moreover, after He raised Lazarus from the dead, Lazarus lived another thirty years and went on to found a church at Kition (now Larnaca), Cyprus. After Lazarus' second death, most of his bones were taken to Constantinople, but it is believed that some fragments that have been unearthed beneath the altar of his church in Larnaca actually belong to the first human in history to be resurrected after having been dead for four days.

Ever since the time of Christ's ministry, Christians have witnessed miracles, believed that a spiritual realm must exist, and consequently, have lost their fear of death and willingly became martyrs for what they had seen and knew to be true. The fact that early Christians saw, believed, and were willing to be martyred for Christ, is evidence that the historicity of miracles is certain. Men and women made the decision to leave their pagan practices and belief systems behind and to lead holy lives. Cowards became brave and were willing to be martyred for the King of Kings and Lord of Lords. A fledgling religion, despite incredible persecution at its outset, took root and rapidly changed the philosophy and politics of the world, indeed, the face of the earth.

CHAPTER TWO ("Miracles Performed by Christ that Prove His Divinity") enumerates 56 miracles that the Lord performed in the chronological order in which the Bible presents them. We begin with the wedding at Cana at which He transformed water into wine. We enumerates the vast and diverse wealth of miracles that He performed during the course of His ministry: He healed the sick; exorcized demons from the possessed; escaped numerous times from the midst of angry mobs that sought to kill Him; prophecized with utmost accuracy His rejection, betrayal, arrest, execution, and resurrection; the elements of nature obeyed Him- He calmed the fierce storm at Galilee, walked on the sea when the wind was violent, cursed the fig tree and it immediately withered away; He fed the multitudes from a few loaves of bread and fish; He enabled Peter to find the Temple tax in a fish's mouth.

CHAPTER THREE ("Miracles Attending His Conception, Birth, Childhood, Crucifixion, Resurrection, and Ascension") enumerates 27 miracles surrounding Christ in chronological order from the angel Gabriels' Annunication to Mary of His Birth to John's prophetic visions of Christ on the island of Patmos. In many of these miracles, angels came to earth from Heaven to carry out a specific mission: Gabriel's Annunciation to Mary; the angel's proclamation of Christ's birth to the shepherds; the angel's warning to Joseph to take Mary and Jesus to Egypt; the angel's instruction to Joseph to return to Israel, but to turn away from Judea. We also enumerate miracles that occurred during Christ's Crucifixion that heralded to the world that He is truly the Son of God: the sky became dark for three hours; the curtain in the Temple was torn in two; there was an earthquake and the rocks were split; the most astounding miracle of all: the graves were opened and the bodies of OT saints arose and were seen by many in Jerusalem. We also enumerate the ten appearance of the Risen Lord after His Ascension: His appearance to Paul, Ananias, Stephen, and John.

CHAPTER FOUR ("Signs in the Temple 30 AD-70 AD") discusses five great miracles that God performed in the Temple in Jerusalem to demonstrate that something had changed in the relationship between man and God. Both Talmuds, the Palestianian Talmud (also known as the Jerusalem Talmud) and the Babylonian Talmud, record that during the years 30 AD-70 AD, miracles transpired that directly related to the atonement of sin, forgiveness, animal sacrifice, and man's accessibility to God. These miracles are the Miracle of the Lots, the Miracle of the Crimson Cloth, the Miracle of the Crimson Thread, the Miracle of the Temple Doors, and the Miracle of the Temple Menorah. These five miracles, taken together, indicate that the

Lamb of God had come to earth and that animal sacrifice was no longer required. We find it significant that the two Talmuds record that the miracles began in the year 30 AD. The Orthodox Church holds that the Lord was crucified in the year 33 AD. Therefore, these signs alerted people during the 3 ½ years of the Lord's ministry, while He was still with us in the flesh, that the significance of Yom Kippur (the Day of Atonement) had changed.

CHAPTER FIVE ("The Miracle of the Holy Flame") recounts the most stunning miracle on the planet earth, one that is rarely discussed in the West. God proves the historicity of Christ's Resurrection every year when He causes the candles to miraculously light on Holy Saturday in the Church of the Resurrection (the Holy Sepulcher) in Jerusalem. Each year, after Christ's tomb has been inspected and sealed with wax by representatives of the Israeli government (to reenact the soldiers guarding the tomb), the Patriarch of Jerusalem enters it with an unlit candle. Thousands of Eastern Orthodox pilgrims travel to the site, also holding unlit candles, awaiting the miracle that is expected to happen. Indeed, this is the place where Heaven meets earth: each year God proves Christ's triumphant victory over death. The Miracle of the Holy Flame is chronicled as far back as 870 AD by the French monk Bernard in his itinerary. After prayer, the Patriarch of Jerusalem passes his unlit candle over the Lord's tomb and it miraculously lights. On some years, the pilgrims unlit candles also miraculously light at precisely that moment. The Holy Spirit moves about the Sepulcher lighting the candles, first on one side, then on the other. The Orthodox await this miracle and they have come to expect it. Christ is faithful to the Church, His earthly bride. Seekers of truth can journey there to see for themselves. Many have and as a result, understand that this is a sign that the Orthodox Church is the true Church of Christ on earth.

The authentic fruits of the Church are miracles performed by His saints as well as their incorruptible relics that emanate the scent of sweet perfume. In **CHAPTER SIX** ("Miracles Performed by the Saints") we examine miracles effected by angels and humans. We begin with the miracles of healing that the Archangel Michael performed at Chairotopa and Colossae in the mid-first century AD. There are three Greek texts, a Latin revision, and an Ethiopian text that attest to Michael's intervention in human affairs. At Chairotopa Michael caused a spring to gush forth that had miraculous healing powers. In addition, he caused an earthquake in order to foil a plan by pagans who plotted to destroy his church sanctuary and healing spring. This is evidence that a causality exists between the persecution of the Orthodox Church and God's intervention in human affairs.

Another early saint, Saint Haralambos, miraculously withstood an endless litany of horrific tortures at the hands of the Roman Emperor Septimius Severus c. 193 AD. His relics have performed many miracles down through the centuries. Saint Theodore the Tyron also withstood cruel punishment at the hands of Roman soldiers who unsuccessfully attempted to convert him to paganism. After Theodore died, his relics have also performed many miracles.

Mary, the Mother of Christ, has performed many miracles throughout the Church age. One such example occurred in 626 AD when Persia attacked the Byzantine Empire. When barbaric hordes of Avers surrounded the city of Constantinople, the Christians inside the walls of the city were trapped. The Patriarch of Constantinople, Sergius I, held an icon of Mary and walked around the periphery of the walls of the city. When the procession was completed, a huge storm with crushing tidal waves came and destroyed the enemy. Afterwards, Christians gathered into a church and sang a hymn to Mary in gratitude and thankfulness. The hymn, called the Akathist Hymn (meaning not seated), has become part of the Orthodox liturgy and is chanted during the weeks preceding Holy Week.

Mary interceded in human affairs again in 1821 when she appeared to a nun, St. Pelagia, in her sleep, on the Aegean island of Tinos. Mary revealed to Pelagia that an icon was buried on the island and gave her instructions as to where to find it. Excavation began and not only was the icon discovered, but in addition, a Byzantine church dedicated to St. John the Baptist was unearthed, and a nearby dry well miraculously filled with water and healed the sick. Today the story is retold in travel books on the Cyclades and tourists go to Tinos to see not only the church that was built there, but the cell in which St. Pelagia lived, as well.

The life of a much beloved saint, Seraphim of Sarov, gives us insight into how to lead a holy life that is pleasing to God. Saint Seraphim was a very humble man who diligently pursued the Kingdom of Heaven. He did everything that the Lord had advised those seeking the Kingdom: he renounced worldly possessions and lived in poverty; he prayed continuously and fasted rigorously; he was quick to forgive and he never held a grudge against those who insulted or assaulted him. A rare man, indeed, Seraphim was brutally attacked by thieves one day with the handle of his own axe. As a result, he walked hunched over the remainder of his life and was forced to use a staff. Nevertheless, he argued clemency for his attackers before a judge. It is also a documented fact that he was always cheerful and that he greeted people warmly, saying, "My joy!" He recognized that giving in to sorrow and depression was giving in to a destructive force and he asked God for the grace to be able to avoid that.

The hallmark of St. Seraphim's life was that he diligently sought the Kingdom of Heaven above all else. Christ had taught, "But seek ye first the kingdom of God, and his righteousness; and all these things shall be added unto you" (Mat 6:33). Seraphim's life is an iconic representation of the truth of the Lord's saying. The gifts that he received from God, clairvoyance and miraculous transfiguration on more than one occasion before witnesses, testify to the truth of this. Because he led a holy and humble life, God loved him and granted him certain gifts. Seraphim did pursue the Kingdom of Heaven, and because of this, the Holy Spirit filled him and miraculously transfigured him into dazzling, brilliant light, much as the Lord had been on Mount Tabor.

His disciple, Nicholas Motovilov, had posed the question, "What is the purpose of the Christian life?" The *staretz* replied, "The true aim of our Christian life, is to acquire the Holy Spirit of God." The disciple asked, "How can I myself recognize His true manifestation?" It was then that both Seraphim and Motovilov were miraculously transfigured into pure light and that their souls were filled with the peace and joy that only Christ brings. The Lord had said, "Peace I leave with you, my peace I give unto you: not as the world giveth, give I unto you" (John 14:27).

No one can read the biography of St. Seraphim without being forever transformed by it: it is an essay in how to lead a life that is pleasing to God; how to realize the Kingdom of Heaven in this life; what kind of a personality one must have and what kind of a life one must lead to invite the Holy Spirit to draw near and make His presence manifest in the physical realm. The reader understands that it takes a strong-willed person, one who, like Seraphim, diligently seeks the Kingdom of Heaven above all else; one who renounces worldly possessions; one who prays and fasts continuously; one who is quick to forgive even those who brutalize him beyond recognition and leave him permanently crippled; one who avidly reads the Bible, applies it to his own life, and faithfully obeys Christ's words.

Seraphim's life teaches us that miracles are the result of the close relationship between God and man. They are evidence of the presence of the Holy Spirit. It is up to man to seek first the Kingdom of Heaven and to make the sacrifices necessary to achieve it.

CHAPTER SEVEN ("Miracles on Mt. Athos") discusses divine intervention on one of the holiest sites in all Christendom. Mt. Athos, the easternmost of three promontories of the Chaldice peninsula that extends into the Aegean Sea, is the site of 20 Orthodox monasteries and houses some of the most treasured and revered artifacts of all Christendom. Many of the invaluable treasures that it houses are the gifts of Byzantine emperors. For example, Mt. Athos holds the largest piece of the True Cross discovered by Saint Helena, a portion of the reed that carried vinegar and gall to the lips of Christ when He was crucified, the skull of St. John Chrysostom, the boxes that held the frankincense, gold, and myrrh that the three Magi presented to the Infant Jesus, and many icons that gush forth human tears, blood, and holy oil. In addition, the monks have been visited by angels, have had visions, and most, if not all of the monks, have been canonized as saints and have performed miracles after they have gone to sleep in the Lord.

Among the innumerable miracles that have occurred on Mt. Athos there is the appearance of the Archangel Gabriel in front of the icon of Axion Esti. On June 11, 980 AD, a group of monks held an all-night vigil in the Holy Dormition Cathedral in Karyes, Mt. Athos. They sang a hymn, "Axion Esti," to the Virgin Mary. However, a new monk appeared among them, one whom they had never seen before, who sang the hymn and added new words at the beginning of it. He identified himself as the Archangel Gabriel, instructed them to add the new words to the hymn at the beginning, and then miraculously vanished from their midst. Since then Axion Esti has been chanted throughout the Orthodox world just as Archangel Gabriel had instructed the monks in the 10th century.

CHAPTER EIGHT ("Miracles Authenticated by the Orthodox Church in the News") recounts several modern day miracles beginning with the Weeping Icon of Mary at St. Nicholas Albanian Orthodox Church, Chicago, IL, in 1986. Because many of the newspapers and some television shows have covered miracles of healing performed by weeping icons of Mary and Jesus or the incorruptible relics of saints, the chapter is prefaced by a lengthy discussion of why icons are important in Orthodox worship. In order to understand why God performs miracles of healing through icons and relics, it is necessary to place living man in the perspective of a timeless eternity in which the soul is immortal, saints realize union with God after they leave their corruptible physical bodies, and continue to interact with humanity from the spiritual realm. Christ said, "God is not the God of the dead, but of the living" (Mat 22:32; Mark 12:27; Luke 20:38). He conquered spiritual death on the Cross on behalf of fallen humanity and therefore those that He has redeemed continue their existence in Heaven and intercede for humanity. Therefore, Chapter Eight begins with a discussion of topics that are basic to understanding why God uses icons to perform miracles: the fact that the Son of God became man so that men might become the sons of God; the fact that the Lord's Transfiguration on Mount Tabor was a foreshadowing of man's theosis; the fact that icons depict the saints who have achieved theosis; the fact that the liturgy itself is a foreshadowing of Heaven; the fact that Mary and the saints are revered precisely because they have achieved theosis or union with God. Once we see that it is God's purpose that Christ should be the firstborn in Heaven among many and that it is His plan that we should all eventually achieve union with Him, then it is easy to understand why miracles occur. The life of the Christian is an endless, eternal continuum. Paul instructed that those who are absent from the body are present with the Lord" (2 Cor 5:8). Therefore, the saints who precede us in Heaven are fully capable of interacting with us if it is God's will. Many modern day miracles are those in which icons of Mary holding the Infant Jesus gush human tears, blood or holy oil. When this happens, many miracles of healing occur and also other icons or picture cards of icons that touch the miraculous icons also begin to stream tears, blood or holy oil and perform miracles of healing. In chronological order we discuss authenticated miracles that have received international coverage in the media: the weeping icon of St. Nicholas Albanian Orthodox Church, Chicago, IL, featured on the Leeza Show; the instance in which blood gushed forth from communion bread in Zarka, Jordan; the weeping icon of St. George Antiochian Orthodox Church, Cicero, IL; the blinking and weeping icon of Christ in the Church of the Nativity, Bethlehem, West Bank, that was covered by Associated Press Television; the weeping icon of Kykko Monastery, Cyprus; the icon card that gushed holy oil at the home of Sam and Salwa Najjar, Schiller Park, IL; and the miracles of healing performed by the incorruptible relics of St. Alexander of Svir.

As Blaise Pascal once argued, if skeptics require empirical evidence that God and Heaven exist, miracles are it!

CHAPTER ONE

Christ's Power to Resurrect the Dead[1]

...he cried with a loud voice, Lazarus, come forth. And he that was dead came forth, bound hand and foot with graveclothes: and his face was bound about with a napkin. Jesus saith unto them, Loose him, and let him go.

—John 11:43-44

Among Christ's greatest miracles were those in which He resurrected the dead. He did this a number of times, both during His ministry and after He surrendered His Ghost on the Cross. There are five instances in the NT in which Christ resurrected the dead (including Himself) and if we address them in chronological order, we will see that a pattern arises in which the glorification of God gradually increases and reaches a crescendo. In the first example, Christ resurrected a woman's son at Nain. She was a widow and she was mourning the loss of her only son.

---

1   Copyright © 2008 from *An Eastern Orthodox View of Pascal* by Mary Efrosini Gregory. Reprinted by permission of Light & Life Publishing Company.

When the bier of the young man was brought to Jesus, He touched it and said, "Young man, I say unto thee, Arise." The man sat up in the coffin and began to speak (Luke 7:11-17). Christ also raised Jairus' twelve year old daughter from the dead (Mat 9:24-25, Mark 5:39-42, Luke 8:49-55). Another resurrection took place when Christ raised his beloved friend, Lazarus, from the dead. After his resurrection, Lazarus went on to found a church in Kition, Cyprus (now Larnaca) and he lived another thirty years. The Eastern Orthodox Church believes that remains discovered beneath the altar of the Church of Saint Lazarus in Larnaca belong to Lazarus and that therefore, this site bears physical evidence of the first man in human history to be resurrected and to die again after he had already been dead and buried for four days. This burial site is held as physical proof of Christ's power to resurrect the dead and therefore, of His divinity.

A fourth example of the resurrection of the dead occurred immediately after Christ surrendered His Ghost on the Cross. The apostle Matthew tells us that the bodies of many OT saints who had died arose and were seen by many in Jerusalem. Since this is an apocalyptic event in human history, let us examine a literal translation of the original Greek text: "And the tombs were opened and many bodies of the saints having fallen asleep were raised, and having gone out from the tombs after the resurrection of him they entered into the holy city and they appeared to many" (Mat 27:52-53).[1] In this powerful statement, Matthew informs us that the graves of OT saints, such as Abraham and Sarah, must be empty today. These graves are well guarded and no one is allowed to open them to see whether they still contain the remains of those who had died. However, physical evidence of the veracity of Matthew's account of the resurrection of OT saints does reside in the tombs of Abraham and Sarah and one only need open them to verify the miracle that God had done immediately after Christ surrendered His Ghost on the Cross. Christ had journeyed to *sheol* and released the OT saints who had died before His advent. In Hebrew *sheol* means "the abode of the dead." It is the Semitic equivalent to the Greek concept of Hades. Christians consider it to be the destination of the dead prior to Christ's Resurrection. *Strong's Concordance* indicates that *sheol* appears 31 times in the OT when the KJV translates it as "hell" and another 30 times when the KJV translates it as "grave." The meaning of *sheol* can be readily inferred from Ps 16:10: "For thou will not leave my soul in *sheol*; neither wilt thou suffer thine Holy One is see corruption." This verse is helpful in understanding what *sheol* means because we see that it is a place where the soul goes. The sentence is divided into two parts: in the first half, the soul goes to *sheol*; in the second, the physical part, the flesh, suffers corruption. We see a division of the parts of the person after death. This verse can be understood on at least three levels: the surface level and two deeper levels. On the surface, the psalmist, David, is confident that when he dies, his soul will not remain in *sheol*, but that His Savior will release him and take him to Heaven. On a deeper level, this verse is a prophecy of the Resurrection of Christ. In addition, it is also a prophecy of Mat 27:52-53 in which Christ releases the OT saints from *sheol*. We can be confident that the grave of David is empty and that God raised him after Christ surrendered His Ghost on the Cross and resurrected "many bodies of the saints having fallen asleep."

Paul advises, since the Lord was the first to rise from the dead and because He set free the souls in *sheol* that had been awaiting Him, believers in Christ can be certain that when they die they will be with Him: "Therefore we are always confident, knowing that, whilst we are at home in the body, we are absent from the Lord" (2 Cor 5:6) and "We are confident, I say, and willing rather to be absent from the body, and to be present with the Lord (2 Cor 5:8). There are only two possibilities for the follower of Christ: either he is in the body or else he is with the Lord. That is because "to be absent in the body is to be present with the Lord."

Finally, the fifth, greatest and most significant resurrection was that of Christ Himself, which occurred, not coincidentally, on the Feast of the First Fruits. The fact that He had gone to *sheol* (Hades) and released OT believers who had died before His Advent and Crucifixion, was proven by the fact that there were many in Jerusalem who saw resurrected dead people and also, many who saw the resurrected Christ.

The resurrection of Christ was prophesied in the OT, was predicted by Christ, Himself, and was witnessed by more than five hundred people at one time, including the apostles (1 Cor 15:6). The fact that men and women became courageous and were willing to die for what they had observed and knew to be true is evidence of the transformative power that His Resurrection had on all who saw Him. Early believers who had seen the resurrection of the dead, the healing of the sick, and the Risen Lord, lost their fear of death and were certain of immortality, despite the imminent thread of persecution.

A good place to begin an examination of Christ's miracles is Mat 9 because this chapter begins with His healing of the sick and includes His resurrection of a young girl from the dead. Matthew takes care to point out that the Lord's healing was intimately intertwined with the forgiveness of sin. He also notes that there was a certain ruler of the synagogue who prostrated himself before Him in adoration and asked for the resurrection of his little girl who had died; Christ, in his compassion, granted the man's prayer. Mark and Luke tells us that this ruler's name was Jairus.

Matthew begins chapter 9 by recalling that Christ healed a man sick with the palsy (Mat 9:2-7). The *OED* defines "palsy" as "paralysis or paresis (weakness) of all or part of the body, sometimes with tremor."[2] In the six verses that comprise Mat 9:27, we have five declarations of Christ's divinity. The first occurs just prior to the paralytic's healing. Jesus declares, "Be of good cheer; thy sins be forgiven thee" (Mat 9:2). He made it clear that he had the authority to forgive sin and this was an affirmation of His deity. The scribes understood the significance of this (God alone has the authority to forgive sin) and they said among themselves that this was blasphemy. Jesus knew what they were thinking and asked, "Wherefore think ye evil in your hearts? For whether is easier to say, Thy sins be forgiven thee; or to say, Arise, and walk?" (Mat 9:4-5). The question, "Wherefore, think ye evil in your hearts?" is a second declaration of His divinity for two reasons. First, he demonstrated that he knew what they were thinking and what was in their hearts. Secondly, he held that equating His forgiveness of sin with blasphemy is intrinsically evil because it refuses to acknowledge His divine nature. The equation forgiveness=blasphemy is intrinsically flawed and evil because it is a conscious denial of Christ's divine nature. Thirdly, Christ acknowledges that His forgiveness is just as easy to grant as is His healing because He is God. He can rearrange the physical matter in a person's body and make him whole because He is God incarnate. Therefore, He has the authority to forgive sin. The apostle John will tell us that He created everything that there is and that there is nothing which is that he did not create (John 1:3). Fourthly, Jesus explains, "But that ye may know that the Son of man hath power on earth to forgive sins…" Fifthly, Jesus commands the sick man, "Arise, take up thy bed, and go unto thine house." Matthew tells us that when the multitudes saw the miracles, they marveled and glorified God.

In Mat 9:9 Jesus is walking past the customs table and calls Matthew. Matthew was a customs officer and tax collector. Jesus said only two words: "Follow me." Matthew informs us that at that moment he arose from the customs table (he left his job) and followed the Lord; Matthew traveled with Him during His 3½ year ministry.

Jesus went to Matthew's house and sat down to eat with tax collectors and sinners. When His disciples were asked why He was dining with tax collectors and sinners, Jesus heard the question and declared, "I am not come to call the righteous, but sinners to repentance" (Mat 9:13). Hence, He points out that all have sinned and have fallen short of the glory of God. Christ came to minister unto those who had the humility to admit that they were sinners. All that was required was for the individual to own up to the fact that he was a sinner in need of forgiveness: Christ always forgave those who asked for forgiveness. Hence, the statement, "I am not come to call the righteous" is a statement that recognizes that man has free will: either he can declare himself to be perfect or else he can admit that he has shortcomings and that he needs to be forgiven.

Then Christ makes a series of prophecies. First, He is asked why the Pharisees fast and His disciples do not. He responds, "Can the children of the bridechamber mourn, as long as the bridegroom is with them? but the days will come, when the bridegroom shall be taken from them, and then shall they fast" (Mat 9:15). This is a prediction of His own execution. Furthermore, the metaphors of bride and bridegroom recur throughout the NT. The Church is metaphorized as the bride of Christ. The metaphors bride, bride chamber or bridegroom appear in Mat 9:15; 25:1; 25:5-6; 25:10; Mark 2:19-20; Luke 5:34-35; 3:29; Rev 21:2; 21:9; 22:17. These metaphors imply faithfulness, protection and concern about the people of God. In human relationships, marriage implies the extension of ego boundaries so that both parties are concerned about the happiness and welfare of each other. The marriage metaphor provides a hint, an allusion to the ultimate theosis or union with God that awaits every believer. Just as in Gen 2:24 Adam and Eve become a unity, one flesh, so also in theosis, Christians will one day achieve spiritual union with God. Orthodox teaching on theosis will be discussed more fully in Chapter 6. He prophesizes the fasting that will take place during Lent for two millennia in remembrance of His Passion and Crucifixion.

Following the metaphorization of God's people as the bride of Christ, He makes a declaration of the New Covenant and distinguishes it from the Old Covenant: "No man putteth a piece of new cloth unto an old garment, for that which is put in to fill it up taketh from the garment, and the rent is made worse. Neither do men put new wine into old bottles: else the bottles break, and the wine runneth out, and the bottles perish: but they put new wine into new bottles, and both are preserved" (Mat 9:16-17). Here the Old Covenant is metaphorized both as an old garment and an old wine bottle; the New Covenant is likened to a piece of new cloth that is used to make a new garment and also to a new wine bottle. He makes it clear that from that moment on that the covenant that God made with Abraham had metamorphosed into its fullness. Christ is the fulfillment of the Law and all the promises that God made to humanity through His prophets.

This is in fulfillment of the prophecy uttered by the prophet Jeremiah: "Behold, the days come, saith the LORD, that I will make a new covenant with the house of Israel, and with the house of Judah: Not according to the covenant that I made with their fathers in the day that I took them by the hand to bring them out of the land of Egypt...But this shall be the covenant that I will make with the house of Israel; After those days, saith the LORD, I will put my law in their inward parts, and write it in their hearts; and will be their God, and they shall be my people. And they shall teach no more every man his neighbour, and every man his brother, saying Know the LORD: for they shall all know me, from the least of them unto the greatest of them, saith the LORD: for I will forgive their iniquity, and I will remember their sin no more" (Jer 31:31-34).

At this point a ruler of a synagogue came forward and worshipped Christ. Matthew says, "...there came a certain ruler, and worshipped him..." (Mat 9:18). The original Greek uses the verb *proskineo* [προσκυνέω], meaning to prostrate oneself in homage, reverence, adoration, worship. The *OED* defines "prostrate" thus: "In strict use, Lying with the face to the ground, in token of submission or humility"[3] While the KJV says, "and worshipped him," the Greek word is much more graphic and indicates that the ruler of the synagogue, who must have been thoroughly acquainted with Hebrew Scriptures and prophecies that the healing of the sick would occur during the Messianic age, humbly prostrated himself on the ground in adoration of the Lord.

Proskineo is used again, most descriptively, to describe the adoration of the three magi before the infant Jesus: "And when they were come into the house, they saw the young child with Mary his mother, and fell down, and worshipped him: and when they had opened their treasures, they presented unto him gifts; gold, and frankincense, and myrrh" (Mat 2:11). Here, *proskineo*, to worship, is preceded by "fell down"; the tautology hyperbolizes the great humility that the magi had and that they recognized Him as a king. Also, in the following verse, *proskineo* is preceded by "falling down on his face": "And thus are the secrets of his heart made manifest; and so falling down on his face he will worship God, and report that God is in you..." (1 Cor 14:25). Again, the tautology of "falling down on his face" and *proskineo* hyperbolizes the act of worshipping God. This form of worship is also seen in Heaven before Christ: "And the four and twenty elders, which sat before God on their seats, fell upon their faces, and worshipped God" (Rev 11:16).

The Greek language also has two other words meaning "worship": *latreo* [λατρεύω] and *sevomai* [σέβομαι]. *Latreo* [λατρεύω] means to pay homage, to worship. It is used in Phil 3:3, which says, "For we are the circumcision, which worship God in the spirit, and rejoice in Christ Jesus, and have no confidence in the flesh." Here, worship is used in the general sense and does not graphically illustrate the act of lying face down on the ground. In fact, "worship God in the spirit" denotes a spiritual adoration, not a physical act. The other Greek word for worship, *sevomai* [σέβομαι], means to revere, to adore, to worship. It is used in Acts 18:7, in which the apostle Paul "entered into a certain man's house, named Justus, one that worshipped God, whose house joined hard to the synagogue." Again, *sevomai*, like *latreo*, means worship in the general sense and does not connote physical prostration. Hence, the original Greek in Mat 9:18, that specifies that the ruler of the synagogue fell on the ground in prostration, tells us that the Father had revealed to him the divinity of Christ. Mark and Luke tell us that the man's name was Jairus.

The Father in Heaven had opened this man's eyes and had revealed to him that Christ was God incarnate on earth. When the faithful came to Christ and asked for help, He never turned them away. This man, who worshipped Him, made the ultimate declaration of faith: he declared that he believed that Christ had the power to resurrect the dead. The man said, "My daughter is even now dead: but come and lay thine hand upon her, and she shall live" (Mat 9:18). This declaration also indicates that Jairus recognized Christ's divine nature: only God can raise the dead. Hence, the fact that he worshipped him and his confidence that Christ could resurrect his daughter from the dead are two signs that he acknowledged Christ to be God Incarnate.

When Jesus entered the ruler's house, he found that there were professional mourners there making noise and playing the flute. The flute players were professional musicians hired to play in mourning ceremonies; the noisy crowd was comprised of mourners who were hired to wail and lament. When Jesus said, "The maid is not dead, but sleepeth," the musicians and professional mourners in the house scornfully laughed and mocked Him. Jesus had them removed from the house and then "he went in, and took her by the hand, and the maid arose" (Mat 9:25). Matthew informs us that His fame spread throughout the whole land.

The other gospel writers also relate this story, but include other details (Mark 5:39-42; Luke 8:49-55). Mark tells us that the father was the ruler of the synagogue and that the people in the house were weeping and wailing greatly. Christ put the visitors out, took the father, mother, and those that were in His company, and entered where the girl was lying. Mark tells us that Christ took her by the hand and said, "Talitha Cumi," which, in Aramaic, means, "Damsel, I say unto thee, arise." The girl immediately arose and walked; she was twelve years old Christ commanded that she be given something to eat.

Luke's account of the miracle provides more information. Christ said, "Fear not: believe only, and she shall be made whole." Here we have the command not to fear and also a statement as to the direct causality between belief and cure. We are also told that He allowed only Peter, James, John, and the parents of the girl to enter the house. The mourners that were there scornfully laughed when He said, "Weep not; she is not dead, but sleepeth" and he removed them from the house. He took her by the hand and commanded, Maid, arise," "and her spirit came again, and she arose straightway."

Matthew informs us that after Jesus performed this miracle and left the ruler's home, He healed two blind men (Mat 9:27). He asked them, "Do you believe that I am able to do this?" They replied, "Yes, Lord," and he restored their vision. This event, along with many other times when He restored vision to the blind, were a fulfillment of Isaiah's prophecy that during the Messianic age, the blind will see, the deaf will hear, the lame will leap like deer, and the mute will shout with joy (Is 35:5).

A third resurrection of the dead and a striking testimony as to the divine nature of Christ occurred when He restored His friend Lazarus to life (John 11:1-44; 12:10-11; Acts 11:19). Lazarus and his sisters, Martha and Mary, lived in Bethany. The apostle John, who traveled with the Lord during His 3 ½ year ministry and who witnessed the raising of Lazarus from the dead, informs us, "Now a certain man was sick, named Lazarus, of Bethany, the town of Mary and his sister Martha. (It was that Mary which anointed the Lord with ointment, and wiped his feet with her hair, whose brother Lazarus was sick.)" and "Now Jesus loved Martha, and her sister, and Lazarus (John 11:1-2, 5).

Lazarus was not only sick, he was dying. When Jesus was told this, He replied, "This sickness is not unto death, but for the glory of God, that the Son of God might be glorified thereby" (John 11:4). Two days later, Jesus informed the apostles, "Our friend Lazarus sleepeth; but I go, that I may awake him out of sleep" (John 11:11). Jesus used the term "sleep" in the metaphoric sense, but the apostles thought that He meant that Lazarus was resting. Then Jesus spoke to them plainly, "Lazarus is dead."

We can consider the raising of Lazarus to be an eyewitness account on the part of the apostle John. John informs us that Jesus was traveling with His disciples when He was told that Lazarus was sick: "Then after that saith he to his disciples, Let us go into Judaea again" (John 11:7). Since Jesus was traveling with His disciples and John relates the events that occurred, we have every reason to believe that John's testimony is his own eyewitness account.

By the time the Lord arrived at Bethany, Lazarus had been buried for four days. When Martha had heard that Jesus was on the way to her house, she ran out and met Him along the way. She declared, "Lord, if thou hadst been here, my brother had not died. But I know, that even now, whatsoever thou wilt ask of God, God will give it thee" (John 11:21-22). Jesus said to her, "Thy brother shall rise again." Martha replied, "I know that he shall rise again in the resurrection at the last day." Jesus said, "I am the resurrection, and the life: he that believeth in me, though he were dead, yet shall he live: And whosoever liveth and believeth in me shall never die. Believest thou this?" Here Martha made an astounding declaration of faith: "Yea, Lord: I believe that thou art the Christ, the Son of God, which should come into the world" (John 11:27). Martha has always been remembered as the one who was busy fixing up her home, while Mary, the wiser of the two, preferred to sit at the Lord's feet and learn (Luke 10:38-41). However, here, we see that Martha was a woman of great faith and that the Father in Heaven had revealed to her the identity of Christ.

Jesus went to the tomb, which was a cave with a stone in front of it. Jesus ordered, "Take ye away the stone." Martha said, "Lord, by this time he stinketh: for he hath been dead four days." Jesus asked her, "Said I not unto thee, that, if thou wouldest believe, thou shouldest see the glory of God?" The stone that was covering the entrance to the cave was removed and then Jesus raised His gaze up to Heaven and thanked the Father for having heard Him. Then He commanded, "Lazarus, come forth." The apostle John informs us, "And he that was dead came forth, bound hand and foot with graveclothes: and his face was bound about with a napkin. Jesus saith unto them, Loose him, and let him go" (John 11:44).

After His execution, many believed and became His followers. However, these early Christians had to flee from Judea because the persecutions began. They traveled throughout the Mediterranean world and founded the original seven churches of Christ that are mentioned in Rev 1 (those in Ephesus, Smyrna, Pergamos, Thyatira, Sardis, Philadelphia, and Laodicea). Mary, the mother of Christ, and the apostle John settled in Ephesus; the resurrected Lazarus, in Cyprus. Paul advises that it was to the Gentiles' great advantage that the setting up of God's kingdom was postponed: the pagan world had not yet been saved and more time was necessary to carry the Good News across the world.

Lazarus fled Judea and went to Cyprus to found a church in Kition, which is now Larnaca. In 52 AD Mary, the mother of Christ, voyaged to Cyprus to visit Lazarus and brought with her a bishop's stole with cuffs that she had woven herself to present to him as a gift.[4] He lived another thirty years after his resurrection and was buried in Kition. In 890 AD Emperor Leo VI erected a magnificent church on his tomb, but carried the remains of Lazarus that he found in a marble sarcophagus to Constantinople. In 1204 the Frank Crusaders captured Constantinople and ransacked the Church of Holy Wisdom (Agia Sophia), carrying many holy things back to Europe with them. The journey of Lazarus' body was traced up to Marseille and then it disappeared.

On Nov. 2, 1972 renovation was being done to the Church of Saint Lazarus in Larnaca and some of his remains were discovered in a marble sarcophagus beneath the altar. These are believed to be genuine; it turns out that the people of Kition had not buried Lazarus all in one place and therefore, they did not surrender all of his relics to Leo VI.

A fifth and pivotal example of the resurrection of the dead is Christ's own Resurrection from the tomb that Joseph of Arimathea had given Him. This resurrection should come as no surprise to anyone well acquainted with Hebrew Scriptures, as it was prophesized many times:

1. "For thou wilt not leave my soul in hell; neither wilt thou suffer thine Holy One to see corruption" (Ps 16:10).
2. "thou hast brought up my soul from the grave: thou hast kept me alive, that I should not go down to the pit" (Ps 30:3).
3. "and his name shall be called...everlasting Father..." (Is 9:6).
4. "And I will preserve thee, and give thee for a covenant of the people..." (Is 49:8).
5. "when thou shalt make his soul an offering for sin, he shall see his seed, he shall prolong his days, and the pleasure of the LORD shall prosper in his hand" (Is 53:10).
6. "After two days will he revive us: in the third day he will raise us up, and we shall live in his sight" (Hos 6:3).
7. "whose goings forth have been from old, from everlasting" (Mic 5:2). This verse is particularly significant because it is a declaration of the awaited Messiah's immortality and hence, of His divinity.

Moreover, Jesus prophesized His own Resurrection many times before His Crucifixion:

1. "For as Jonas was three days and three nights in the whale's belly; so shall the Son of man be three days and three nights in the heart of the earth" (Mat 12:40).
2. "A wicked and adulterous generation seeketh after a sign; and there shall no sign be given unto it, but the sign of the prophet Jonas" (Mat 16:4).
3. "From that time forth began Jesus to show unto his disciples, how that he must go unto Jerusalem, and suffer many things of the elders and chief priests and scribes, and be killed, and be raised again the third day" (Mat 16:21).
4. "And as they came down from the mountain, Jesus charged them saying, Tell the vision to no man, until the

Son of man be risen again from the dead" (Mat 17:9). This occurred after the transfiguration on the mountain; Jesus took Peter, James, and John up a mountain and he was transfigured before them; His face shone as the sun and His clothing was as white light; they saw Moses and Elias talking to the Lord.

5. "And while they abode in Galilee, Jesus said unto them, The Son of man shall be betrayed into the hands of men: And they shall kill him, and the third day he shall be raised again. And they were exceeding sorry" (Mat 17:22-23).

6. "Behold, we go up to Jerusalem; and the Son of man shall be betrayed unto the chief priests and unto the scribes, and they shall condemn him to death, And shall deliver him to the Gentiles to mock, and to scourge, and to crucify him: and the third day he shall rise again" (Mat 20:18-19).

7. "Then saith Jesus unto them, All ye shall be offended because of me this night: for it is written, I will smite the shepherd, and the sheep of the flock shall be scattered abroad. But after I am risen again, I will go before you into Galilee" (Mat 26:31-32).

8. "And he began to teach them, that the Son of man must suffer many things, and be rejected of the elders, and of the chief priests, and scribes, and be killed and after three days rise again" (Mark 8:31).

9. "And they came down from the mountain, he charged them that they should tell no man what things they had seen, till the son of man were risen from the dead. And they kept that saying with themselves, questioning one with another what the rising from the dead should mean" (Mark 9:9-10).

10. "And they were in the way going up to Jerusalem; and Jesus went before them: and they were amazed; and as they followed, they were afraid. And he took again the

twelve, and began to tell them what things should happen unto him, Saying, Behold, we go up to Jerusalem; and the Son of man shall be delivered unto the chief priests, and unto the scribes; and they shall condemn him to death, and shall deliver him to the Gentiles" (Mark 10:32).

11. "Then he took unto him the twelve, and said unto them, Behold, we go up to Jerusalem, and all things that are written by the prophets concerning the son of man shall be accomplished. For he shall be delivered unto the Gentiles, and shall be mocked, and spitefully entreated, and spitted on: And they shall scourge him, and put him to death: and the third day he shall rise again" (Luke 18:31-33).

12. "And his disciples remembered that it was written, The zeal of thine house hath eaten me up. Then answered the Jews and said unto him, What sign showest thou unto us, seeing that thou doest these things? Jesus answered and said unto them, Destroy this temple, and in three days I will raise it up. Then said the Jews, Forty and six years was this temple in building, and wilt thou rear it up in three days? But he spoke of the temple of his body. When therefore he was risen from the dead, his disciples remembered that he had said thus unto them; and they believed the scripture, and the word which Jesus had said" (John 2:17-22).

13. "Therefore doth my Father love me, because I lay down my life, that I might take it again. No man taketh it from me, but I lay it down of myself. I have power to lay it down, and I have power to take it again. This commandment have I received of my Father" (John 10:17-18).

14. "Jesus said unto her, I am the resurrection, and the life: he that believeth in me, though he were dead, yet shall he live: And whosoever liveth and believeth in me shall never die. Believest thou this?" (John 11:25-26).

The risen Lord was witnessed by thousands of people who because they had seen Him, believed, and were willing to die for what they knew to be true. First He appeared to Mary Magdalene in the garden in Jerusalem on Resurrection Sunday (Mark 16:9-11; John 20:11-18); then to Mary, the mother of James, Salome, and Joanna in Jerusalem on Resurrection Sunday (Mat 28:9-10; Mark 16:1; Luke 24:9); to Peter and Cleopas on Resurrection Sunday on the seven mile road from Jerusalem to Emmaus and He discussed Scriptures with them (Mark 16:12; Luke 24:13-35); to Peter (also called Cephas, as *kephas* is Aramaic for "rock") in Jerusalem on Resurrection Sunday (Luke 24:34; 1 Cor 15:5); to the ten assembled disciples in the Upper Room in Jerusalem on Sunday (Mark 16:14; Luke 24:36-49; John 20:19-25); to eleven assembled disciples in the Upper Room in Jerusalem one week later (John 20:26-31); to the doubting Thomas, who touched His pierced hands, put his hand in His pierced side, and believed (John 20:26-29); to seven disciples (Simon, Thomas, Nathaniel, the sons of Zebedee, and two others) while fishing in the Sea of Tiberius (John 21:1-25); to the eleven on a mountain in Galilee (Mat 28:16-20); Mark 16:14-18); to the doubting James (1 Cor 15:7); to the disciples in Jerusalem (Luke 24:36-49); to the disciples who witnessed His ascension to Heaven forty days later from the Mount of Olives (Mat 28:16-20; Mark 16:19-20; Luke 24:50-53; Acts 1:3-11); to Saul of Tarsus on the road to Damascus (Acts 9:1-19; 22:3-16; 26:9-18; 1 Cor 9:1); His voice was heard by the men traveling with Saul (Acts 9:7); He appeared to Ananias (Acts 9:10-16); to more than five hundred people, who saw Him at the same time (1 Cor 15:6).

In Mat 28:9 Jesus met the women who had come to bring Him spices and said, "Rejoice!" The original Greek says, "Χαίρετε." [Rejoice!]. The verb χαίρω means to rejoice, to be of cheer. It is significant that the word is in the imperative: the command implies, "Rejoice! I have conquered death on the Cross; you have everlasting life; there is much to be happy about." The first word that the Lord spoke on the Sunday of His Resurrection has come to mean "hello" and it has been used as a greeting down through the millennia among Greeks.

Endnotes

1   *The New Greek-English Interlinear New Testament*, translated by Robert K. Brown and Philip W. Comfort and edited by J. D. Douglas (Carol Stream: Tyndale House Publishers, Inc., 1993), 114.

2   "Palsy," *Oxford English Dictionary Online*, 1a, http://dictionary.oed.com (Mar. 9, 2007).

3   "Prostrate," *Oxford English Dictionary Online*, 1, http://dictionary.oed.com (Mar. 7, 2007).

4   Father Demetrios Serfes, "St. Lazarus the Friend of Christ and First Bishop of Kition, Cyprus." http://www.serfes.org/lives/stlazarus.htm (Mar. 6, 2007).

CHAPTER TWO

Miracles Performed by Christ that Prove His Divinity[2]

For unto us a child is born, unto us a son is given: and the government shall be upon his shoulder: and his name shall be called Wonderful, Counsellor, The mighty God, The everlasting Father, The Prince of Peace.

—Is 9:6

The apostles Matthew, Mark, Luke, and John provide eyewitness testimony as to the vast wealth of miracles that the Lord performed. John ends his gospel by declaring, "And there are also many other things which Jesus did, the which, if they should be written every one, I suppose that even the world itself could not contain the books that should be written" (John 21:25). Below is an enumeration, in chronological order, of some of the many miracles that Christ performed:

2   Copyright © 2008 from *An Eastern Orthodox View of Pascal* by Mary Efrosini Gregory. Reprinted by permission of Light & Life Publishing Company.

1. performs His first miracle: turns water into wine at the wedding feast at Cana in Galilee (John 2:1-11)
2. prophesizes that He will raise His body three days after His life is taken (John 2:19-22)
3. He miraculously cures someone despite the great distance between Himself and the sick person: while at Cana, He gives the word and heals a nobleman's son who is dying of a fever at Capernaum. When the father returns to Capernaum, he learns that his son recovered from his illness at 7:00 the previous day, precisely the time when the Lord had promised him that his son would be healed (John 4:46-54).
4. "passing through the midst of them," evades a hostile multitude in Nazareth that led Him to the brow of a hill with the intention of pushing Him down a cliff (Luke 4:28-30)
5. enables Peter to catch a first draught of fish (Luke 5: 4-10)
6. exorcizes an unclean spirit from a man in the synagogue at Capernaum on the Sabbath (Mark 1:21-28; Luke 4:31-37)
7. heals Peter's mother-in-law of a fever at Capernaum (Mat 8:14-15; Mark 1:30-31; Luke 4:38-39)
8. lays hands on many sick people and heals them at Capernaum (Mat 8:16-17; Mark 1:32-34; Luke 4:40)
9. exorcizes demons from the possessed at Capernaum (Mat 8:16-17; Mark 1:32-34; Luke 4:41)
10. cleanses a man with leprosy (Mat 8:2-4; Mark 1:40-45; Luke 5:12-14)
11. forgives and heals a paralytic at Capernaum (Mat 9:2; Mark 2:3-12; Luke 5:18-26)
12. heals a man who had been an invalid for 38 years in Jerusalem on the Sabbath (John 5:5-13)
13. restores a man's withered hand and makes it whole in the synagogue on the Sabbath (Mat 12:10-13; Mark 3:1-5; Luke 6:6-10)

14. heals a centurion's servant of the palsy in Capernaum (Mat 8:5-13; Luke 7:1-10)
15. prophesizes that the Gentile world will believe and enter the Kingdom of Heaven: many will come from the east and the west and will sit down with Abraham, Isaac, and Jacob in the Kingdom of Heaven (Mat 8:10-12)
16. raises a widow's son from the dead at Nain; the young man sits up in his bier and begins to speak (Luke 7: 11-15)
17. calms a fierce storm on the sea of Galilee (Mat 8:23-27; Mark 4:35-41; Luke 8:22-25)
18. exorcizes unclean spirits from a demoniac at the Gadarenes; casts the demons into a herd of 2,000 swine that runs down a cliff into the sea and is drowned (Mat 8:28-34; Mark 5:1-20; Luke 8:26-39)
19. heals a woman who has been bleeding for twelve years; she touches the hem of His garment and is restored to health (Mat 9:20-22; Mark 5:25-34; Luke 8:43-48)
20. raises Jairus' daughter from the dead at Capernaum (Mat 9:18-19; 9:23-26; Mark 5:22-24; 5:35-43; Luke 8:41-42; 8:49-56)
21. restores sight to two blind men (Mat 9:27-31)
22. restores speech to a mute and exorcizes a demon from him (Mat 9:32-33)
23. heals every sickness and every disease among the people (Mat 8:35)
24. heals the sick (Mat 14:14; Luke 9:11)
25. given five barley loaves and two small fish, He feeds 5,000 men, besides women and children in a desert in Bethsaida; twelve baskets of fragments are left over (Mat 14:15-21; Mark 6:33-44; Luke 9:12-17; John 6:1-13)
26. walks on the sea when the wind is fierce (Mat 14:22-33; Mark 6:45-52; John 6:16-21)
27. enables Peter to walk on the sea and catches him when his faith waivers (Mat 14:28-32)

28. all the diseased that touch the hem of His garment are healed of their illnesses at Gennesaret (Mat 14:34-36; Mark 6:53-56)

29. exorcizes a demon from the Canaanite woman's daughter (Mat 15:22-28, Mark 7:24-30)

30. heals the lame, the blind, the mute, the maimed, and many others at Decapolis (Mat 15:29-31)

31. restores hearing and speech to a deaf mute at Decapolis (Mark 7:31-37)

32. given seven loaves and a few fish, feeds 4,000 men, besides women and children at Decapolis; seven baskets of broken meat are left over (Mat 15:32-39; Mark 8: 1-9)

33. heals a blind man at Bethsaida (Mark 8:22-26)

34. at Caesarea Philippi, prophesizes for the first time His rejection by the elders, chief priests, and scribes, Crucifixion, and Resurrection after three days (Mat 16: 21-24; Mark 8:31-34; Luke 9:22-23)

35. the transfiguration of Christ: Christ is seen with Moses and Elijah on the mountain (Mat 17:1-9; Mark 9:2-9; Luke 9:28-36)

36. exorcizes demons out of a man's son (Mat 17:14-21; Mark 9:14-29; Luke 9:37-43)

37. prophesizes a second time his death and Resurrection (Mat 17: 22-23; Mark 9:9-10; 9:31-32; Luke 9:43-45)

38. enables Peter to find the Temple tax ($\delta i\delta\rho\alpha\chi\mu\alpha$, a two-drachma piece) in a fish's mouth (Mat 17:24-27)

39. During the Feast of Tabernacles, hostile mobs seek to take Him, but cannot because His hour has not yet come (John 7:30-33; 7:44).

40. evades a hostile multitude that tries to stone Him (John 8:59)

41. heals a man who was born blind in Jerusalem (John 9: 1-41)

42. heals the infirm, bent woman who had been stooped over for 18 years (Luke 13:11-13)
43. evades another hostile multitude in Jerusalem that tries to take Him (John 10:39)
44. prophesizes His death and resurrection on the third day (Luke 13:31-33)
45. heals a man with dropsy (Luke 14:1-4)
46. resurrects Lazarus from the dead at Bethany (John 11:1-44)
47. heals ten lepers while passing through Samaria and Galilee (Luke 17:11-19)
48. while going to Jerusalem, prophecizes for the third time that He will be condemned, delivered to be mocked, scourged and crucified, and that He will be resurrected on the third day (Mat 20:17-19; Mark 10:32-34; Luke 18:31-34)
49. heals the blind Bartimaeus at Jericho (Mat 20:29-34; Mark 10:46-52; Luke 18:35-43)
50. curses the fig tree and it immediately withers away (Mat 21:19; Mark 11:13-14; 11:20-21)
51. identifies Judas as being the one who will betray Him (Mat 26:21-25; Mark 14:18-21; Luke 22:21-23; John 13:21-30)
52. At the Last Supper before His Crucifixion, He transforms wine into His Blood and bread into His Body and prophesizes that this will be the last time that He will taste wine before He drinks it again in Heaven; this is a miracle; it is also a prophesy of His imminent execution; moreover, it is a prophesy that this miracle will continue to be done in His Church until His return (Mat 26:26-29; Mark 14:22-25; Luke 22:16-20; John 6:51-58)
53. predicts Peter's denial of Him (Mat 26:31-35; Mark 14:27-31; Luke 22:31-38; John 13:31-34)
54. prophesizes His Resurrection and the disciples' joy to see Him again (John 16:16-22)

55. restores the ear of Malchus, a servant of the high priest, after Peter draws a sword and cuts it off (Mat 26:51-54; Mark 14:47-49; Luke 22:49-51; John 18:10-11)

56. enables the apostles to catch a second draught of fish (John 21:5-11)[1]

Endnotes

1   This collation has been assembled using the following tools: the cross-references in the *Holy Bible*, KJV (Grand Rapids: Zondervan, 2000); Archibald Thomas Robertson, *A Harmony of the Gospels for Students of the Life of Christ: Based on the Broadus Harmony in the Revised Version* (New York: George H. Doran Company, 1922), 1-252, the list on 294; J.W. McGarvey and Philip Y. Pendleton, *The Fourfold Gospel or A Harmony of the Four Gospels* (Cincinnati: The Standard Publishing Company, 1914), 1-767; the cross-references in the *NIV Study Bible* (Grand Rapids: Zondervan, 2002), and "The Life of Christ" chart on 2010-12 and "The Harmony of the Gospels" table on 2224-29; "Harmony of the Gospels" and "The Miracles of Jesus Christ" in James Strong, ed., *The New Strong's Exhaustive Concordance of the Bible* (Nashville: Thomas Nelson Publishers, 1990), unnumbered, unpaginated appendices.

CHAPTER THREE

Miracles Attending His Conception, Birth, Childhood, Crucifixion, Resurrection, and Ascension[3]

And the graves were opened; and many bodies of the saints which slept arose,
And came out of the graves after his resurrection, and went into the holy city, and appeared unto many.
                                                    —Mat 27:52-53

1. the angel Gabriel's Annunciation to Mary of the Birth of Christ (Luke 1:26-38)
2. an angel of the Lord's Annunciation to Joseph that Mary's Child has been conceived by the Holy Ghost (Mat 1:18-25)

3. an angel of the Lord proclaims the Birth of Jesus to the shepherds; a multitude of angels praises God (Luke 2:8-20)

4. the three magi arrive from the East having followed a star that miraculously appears over His birthplace (Mat 2:1-12)

5. an angel of the Lord warns Joseph in a dream to take Mary and Jesus to Egypt (Mat 2:13-18)

6. an angel of the Lord tells Joseph to bring them back to Israel; Joseph is warned in a dream to turn away from Judea; he goes to Nazareth (Mat 2:19-23; Luke 2:39)

7. At the age of 12 He both hears and asks questions of renown teachers in the Temple in Jerusalem; all that hear Him are astonished at his understanding and answers (Luke 2:42-47). Many believe that Hillel, the foremost scholar of biblical commentary and interpreter of the Law, must have been present in the Temple in Jerusalem on Passover, and that Jesus taught Hillel, it was not the other way around.

8. when Jesus is baptized by John, the Father speaks from Heaven and the Holy Spirit descends like a dove (Mat 3:13-17; Mark 1:9-11; Luke 3:21-23)

9. first miracle attending His Crucifixion: the sky becomes dark for three hours over the whole land (Mat 27:45; Mark 15:33; Luke 23:44)

10. second miracle attending His Crucifixion: the curtain in the Temple is torn in two. This is indeed a miracle of God because it is six inches thick and requires 300 men to carry it (Mat 27:51; Mark 15:38; Luke 23:45)

11. third miracle attending His Crucifixion: the earth was shaken and the rocks were split: "the earth did quake, and the rocks rent...Now the centurion, and they that were with him, watching Jesus, saw the earthquake, and those things that were done..." (Mat 27:51, 54)

12. fourth miracle attending His Crucifixion: the tombs were opened and the dead were resurrected: "And the

graves were opened; and many of the bodies of the saints which slept arose, And came out of the graves after his resurrection, and went into the holy city, and appeared unto many" (Mat 27:52-53)

13. fifth miracle attending His Crucifixion: the Roman centurion, a pagan, is converted and declares, "Truly, this man was the Son of God!" (Mat 27:54; Mark 15:39; Luke 23:47)
14. angels announce the Resurrection to certain women; Peter and John enter the empty tomb (Mat 28:1-8; Mark 16:1-8; Luke 24:1-8; John 20:1-10)
15. first and second appearances of the Risen Lord (Mat 28:9-10; Mark 16:9-11; Luke 24:9-11; John 20:11-18)
16. third and fourth appearances of the Risen Lord (Mark 16:12-13; Luke 24:13-35; 1 Cor 15:5)
17. fifth appearance of the Risen Lord (Mark 16:4; Luke 24:36-43; John 20:19-25)
18. sixth appearance of the Risen Lord (John 20:26-31; 1 Cor 15:5)
19. seventh appearance of the Risen Lord (John 21:1-15)
20. eighth appearance of the Risen Lord (Mat 28:16-17; 1 Cor 15:6)
21. ninth and tenth appearances of the Risen Lord (Luke 24:44-49; Acts 1:3-8; 1 Cor 15:7)
22. the Ascension (Mark 16:19-20; Luke 24:50-53; Acts 1:9-12)
23. first appearance after His Ascension is to Paul (Acts 9:1-9; 22:6-11; 26:12-18; 1 Cor 15:8)
24. second appearance after His Ascension is to Ananias (Acts 1:10-16)
25. third appearance after His Ascension is in a vision to Stephen (Acts 7:55)
26. He speaks to Peter, telling him to eat of all living things (Acts 10:10-16; 11:5-10)
27. vision of John (Rev 1-5; 6:1; 14:1; 22)[1]

Endnotes

1   This collation has been assembled using the following tools: the cross-references in the *Holy Bible*, KJV (Grand Rapids: Zondervan, 2000); Archibald Thomas Robertson, *A Harmony of the Gospels for Students of the Life of Christ: Based on the Broadus Harmony in the Revised Version* (New York: George H. Doran Company, 1922), 1-252, the list on 294; J.W. McGarvey and Philip Y. Pendleton, *The Fourfold Gospel or A Harmony of the Four Gospels* (Cincinnati: The Standard Publishing Company, 1914), 1-767; the cross-references in the *NIV Study Bible* (Grand Rapids: Zondervan, 2002), and "The Life of Christ" chart on 2010-12 and "The Harmony of the Gospels" table on 2224-29; "Harmony of the Gospels" and "The Miracles of Jesus Christ" in James Strong, ed., *The New Strong's Exhaustive Concordance of the Bible* (Nashville: Thomas Nelson Publishers, 1990), unnumbered, unpaginated appendices.

CHAPTER FOUR

Signs in the Temple 30 AD-70 AD[4]

*Behold, the days come, saith the LORD, that I will make a
new covenant with the house of Israel, and with the house of
Judah: Not according to the covenant that I made with their
fathers in the day that I took them by the hand to bring them
out of the land of Egypt...*

—Jer 31:31-32

In addition to the miracles that Christ performed, there
are some stunning miracles that occurred in the Temple
during the years 30 AD-70 AD that the Talmud records.
Centuries after the destruction of the Temple in 70 AD, the Jews
began to write their religious history and commentary in two
works: one was written in Palestine and is called the Palestinian
Talmud or the Jerusalem Talmud (translated orally for centuries
prior to its compilation by Jewish scholars between the 3rd-4th

century); the other is called the Babylonian Talmud (compiled by Jewish scholars about 499 AD, with some later additions). It is significant that both versions of the Talmud indicate that each year during the period 30 AD-70 AD, God provided five great miracles to demonstrate that something had changed in the relationship between man and God. It is the testimony of the Gospel writers who had traveled with Christ during His ministry, the writings of Paul, and the testimony of the early martyrs that explain that this "something" that had changed was the fact that the Lamb of God had come to earth and that animal sacrifice was no longer required. The five miracles that the Talmud records are as follows:

1. The Miracle of the Lots. On the Day of Atonement (Yom Kippur), lots were cast to decide which of two goats would be sacrificed and which would be set free. During this ritual, two goats were brought before the High Priest, as well as a container bearing two stones. One stone was white and was called the "Lot for the Lord"; the other stone was black and was called the "Lot for the Scapegoat." Without looking into the container, the priest reached into it with his right hand, selected a stone, and held it over the goat that was standing on his right hand side. If the stone was white, the goat on the priest's right hand side would be called "For the Lord" and would be sacrificed; the other goat would be called "Azazel" or the scapegoat and would be set free. If the stone was black, the goat on the priest's right hand side would be set free and the other would be sacrificed. The statistical probability that the High Priest would pick either color is 50-50 and history bore this out. During the 200 years before 30 AD, the High Priest picked one color or the other 50 percent of the time. However, beginning in 30 AD and continuing each year until 70 AD, a black stone always turned up in the High Priest's

right hand. The statistical probability of this happening in forty consecutive years is 1:1,099,511,627,776 or more than a trillion to one. The way to calculate the chances of this happening are as follows: the chances of getting one of two colors after one throw are 1:2. The chances of getting the same color after two consecutive throws are 1 in 2x2 or 1:4. The chances of getting the same color after three consecutive throws are 1 in 2x2x2 or 1:8. If we continue on to forty consecutive throws, we get 1: 1,099,511,627,776. The Jews regarded this phenomenon to be a harbinger of ill fortune and they were afraid that something terrible was going to happen.

2. The Miracle of the Crimson Cloth. On Yom Kippur the High Priest dipped a white cloth in the blood of the animal that had been sacrificed and placed this bloody cloth on the door of the Temple overnight. In the morning it was discovered that God had turned the crimson cloth white again, as a sign that He had accepted the animal sacrifice and that the people's sins were covered by it. This miracle has an antecedent reference in Isaiah: "Come now, and let us reason together, saith the LORD: though your sins be as scarlet, they shall be as white as snow; though they be as red as crimson, they shall be as wool" (Is 1:18). However, the Talmud indicates that during the years 30 AD until the destruction of the Temple in 70 AD, this miracle had ceased and the crimson cloth no longer turned white. Christians understand that God was indicating that he had created something new, a New Covenant in which the ritual sacrifice of animals was no longer necessary, and that He required all of humanity to be justified by the blood that removes sin, not merely covers it (as does animal sacrifice), namely, the blood of Christ. The miracle of the crimson cloth ceased forever.

3. The Miracle of the Crimson Thread. On Yom Kippur the High Priest wore a crimson thread into the Temple's

Holy of Holies (the second tabernacle) and God turned the crimson thread white. After 30 AD, this crimson thread never turned white again.

4. The Miracle of the Temple Doors. Beginning in 30 AD, the Temple doors swung open every night by themselves. This continued each night for forty years until 70 AD. This miracle could be interpreted in a few ways. Christians saw this as a sign that humanity could now enter the Holy of Holies and commune with the Living God through our High Priest, Jesus Christ. The Bible tells us that when Christ surrendered His Ghost on the Cross, the veil in the Temple was rent in two. This was, indeed, a miracle performed by God, and not the work of man, because the veil was six inches thick and 300 priests were required to carry it. The tearing of the veil indicated that a human high priest was no longer needed to be the intercessor between the Living God and man. The Living God came to earth and now Christ is our Tabernacle of the Living God. Those who believe in Him are indwelt by the Holy Spirit and have God residing within them. They are born of the Spirit. They can commune directly with the Father through the intercession of the Son. On the other hand, there was another way of interpreting the Miracle of the Temple Doors. This second interpretation need not be considered to be an alternative to the first; both can be accepted concurrently. Some considered this miracle to be an ominous sign because the prophet Zechariah had predicted, "Open thy doors, O Lebanon, that the fire may devour thy cedars" (Zech 11:1). The doors were made of cedars of Lebanon and covered with gold. The entire eleventh chapter of Zechariah describes the judgment that God would one day mete out to Israel. One verse predicts that the people will be smitten by the king of their neighbors: "For I will no more pity the inhabitants of the land, saith the LORD: but, lo, I will deliver the men

every one into his neighbor's hand, and into the hand of his king: and they shall smite the land, and out of their land I will not deliver them" (Zech 11:6). A few verses later Zechariah announces that at this time Israel will suffer the worst punishment of all, cannibalism: "Then said I, I will not feed you: that that dieth, let it die; and that that is to be cut off, let it be cut off; and let the rest eat every one the flesh of another" (Zech 11:9). The Jerusalem Talmud notes that the Miracle of the Temple Doors was regarded as a sign of great impending destruction and devastation: "Said [to the Temple] Rabban Yohanan ben Zakkai, O Temple, why do you frighten us? We know that you will end up destroyed. For it has been said, Open your doors, O Lebanon, that the fire may devour your cedars! (Zech 11:1)."[1]

5. The Miracle of the Temple Menorah. After Christ's Crucifixion, the seven candlestick menorah in the Temple self-extinguished every night for forty years (on over 12,500 consecutive nights). This happened every night despite the precautions that the priests took to keep the candles lit.

Now let us examine the passages in both the Jerusalem Talmud and the Babylonian Talmud that cite these miracles. The Jerusalem Talmud states, "It has been taught: Forty years before the destruction of the Temple the western light went out, the crimson thread remained crimson, and the lot for the Lord always came up in the left hand. They would close the gates of the Temple by night and get up in the morning and find them wide open. Said [to the Temple] Rabban Yohanan ben Zakkai, O Temple, why do you frighten us? We know that you will end up destroyed. For it has been said, Open your doors, O Lebanon, that the fire may devour your cedars! (Zech. 11:1)."[2] The Babylonian Talmud states, "Our Rabbis taught: During the last forty years before the destruction of the Temple the lot ['For the Lord'] did not come up in the right hand; nor did the crimson-coloured strap become white; nor did the westernmost light shine; and the doors of the *Hekal* would open by themselves, until R. Johanan b. Zakkai rebuked them, saying: *Hekal, Hekal,* why wilt thou be the alarmer thyself? I know about thee that thou wilt be destroyed, for Zechariah ben Ido has already prophesied concerning thee: *Open thy doors, O Lebanon, that the fire may devour thy cedars.*"[3]

It is significant that both Talmuds indicate that these astonishing Temple miracles commenced in 30 AD: the Lord began His 3 ½ year ministry in 30 AD. Hence, God was alerting man that it was time to take the next step in the unfolding of the God-man relationship (which would ultimately lead to theosis or unification with God): the King of Kings and Lord of Lords had arrived in the flesh to forgive sins in person. Prior to healing people, He forgave them their sins. Hence, the start of the Temple miracles in 30 AD indicated that the Tabernacle of the Living God had come to earth and that the forgiveness of sin had begun. God's plan for man's redemption reached its fulfillment when Christ declared, just prior to surrendering His Ghost on the Cross, *tete'lestai* (τετέλεσται) (the original Greek text, John 19:30), which is an accounting term meaning "the debt has been paid in full." Christ's sacrifice, in our place for our transgressions, did not merely cover men's sins, as animal sacrifice had done, but took them away forever, in fulfillment of the prophecy, "As far as the east is from the west, so far hath he removed our transgressions from us" (Ps 103:12).

It is highly significant that God uttered this word prior to leaving us and an examination of its meaning reveals why He chose a language as rich and as vast as Greek in which to record the events of His sojourn on earth. Liddell and Scott's *A Greek-English Lexicon* indicates that τετέλεστο, a form of τελέω, means "fulfill one's word...*to be fulfilled*...pay what one owes, what is due...esp. tax, duty, toll...Pass. Of money, etc., *to be paid*...bring to an end, finish…lay out, spend."[4] Hence, the Lord's words on the Cross, in the original Greek, means three things that all have immense theological significance. First, the word does mean "It is finished," as the KJV translation indicates. Christ accomplished His mission on earth and realized all of the OT prophecies that had been written about Him. Secondly, it means "the debt has been paid in full." Τετέλεσται is an accounting term meaning that a debt or obligation has been fully paid. The obligation here is Christ's payment in full, for each believer's sins. This is in fulfillment of the prophecy dating back to God's exhortation to the snake in the Garden of Eden: "And I will put enmity between thee and the woman, and between thy seed and her seed; it shall bruise thy head, and thou shalt bruise his heel" (Gen 3:15). The surface level meaning of this verse (*p'shat*) is that the snake must crawl on his belly and be subject to being stepped on by humans. However, on a deeper level (*sod*), it is a Messianic prophecy: Christ, a descendant of Eve, will conquer spiritual death on the Cross and proclaim victory over the powers of darkness. He will forgive the sins of Adam and Eve and once more give humanity the opportunity to enter God's kingdom. Paul reiterates this in Rom 16:20. Thirdly, τετέλεσται means "the word has been fulfilled," "the word has been kept." Christ has kept his promise, indeed. Is 6:8 reads, "And I heard the voice of the Lord, saying, Whom shall I send, and who will go for us? Then said I, Here am I; send me." On the surface level, (*p'shat*), Isaiah is offering to carry God's message to man. On a deeper level (*sod*), God is having a Divine Counsel in Heaven and Christ is offering to do the will of the Father, and condescend to go to earth and suffer and die in our place, for our transgressions. He kept His promise: His word, "Here am I; send me," has been kept. Moreover, His promise in Is 61:1 has also been kept: "The Spirit of the Lord GOD is upon me; because the LORD hath anointed me to preach good tidings unto the meek; he hath sent me to bind up the brokenhearted, to proclaim liberty to the captives, and the opening of the prisons to them that are bound."

Luke tells us that at the outset of His ministry, Jesus stood in the synagogue in Nazareth on the Sabbath day and read Is 61:1 (Luke 4:16-21). Then he closed the book, sat down to teach and announced to the congregation that on that day this scripture was fulfilled: "This day is this scripture fulfilled in your ears." This statement had incalculable significance in human history: Christ was revealing that the Holy Spirit was upon Him, that the Holy Spirit had anointed Him to preach the gospel to the poor; that the Holy Spirit had sent Him to heal the brokenhearted, to proclaim liberty to captives (those in bondage to sin), give sight to the blind (both physically and spiritually), to free those held bound in prisons (again, meaning held in bondage to sin). Hence, when he said, "*Τετέλεσται*," "the word has been kept," He was declaring that He had kept His word and accomplished all of the things that He had promised that He would do.

Endnotes

1   *Yoma*, 6:3, in *The Talmud of the Land of Israel: A Preliminary Translation and Explanation*, translated by Jacob Neusner (Chicago: The University of Chicago Press, 1990), 14:176.

2   Ibid.

3   *Yoma*, 39b, in *Seder Mo'ed*, 4 vols., in *The Babylonian Talmud, Translated into English with Notes, Glossary and Indices under the Editorship of Rabbi Dr I. Epstein, Seder Mo'ed*, (London: The Soncino Press, 1938), 3:186.

4   "Τετέλεσται," *A Greek-English Lexicon*, edited by Henry George Liddell and Robert Scott, revised and unabridged (Oxford: Clarendon Press, 1958), 1772.

CHAPTER FIVE

The Miracle of the Holy Flame[5]

*And Jesus came and spake unto them, saying, All power is
given unto me in heaven and in earth. Go ye therefore, and
teach all nations, baptizing them in the name of the Father,
and of the Son, and of the Holy Ghost: Teaching them to
observe all things whatsoever I have commanded you: and,
lo, I am with you always, even unto the end of the world.*

—Mat 28:18-20

A great new miracle took place that demonstrated to the
whole world that Christ is truly risen, and this miracle
has been continuing for 2,000 years: when the Greek
Orthodox Patriarch of Jerusalem passes his unlit candle across
the tomb of Christ on Holy Saturday, it miraculously lights. The
miracle of the Holy Flame is well known and well documented
both in Church history and in the present day.

5   Copyright © 2008 from *An Eastern Orthodox View of Pascal* by Mary Efrosini Gregory. Reprinted
by permission of Light & Life Publishing Company.

The miracle of the Holy Flame is chronicled in the 9th century itinerary of the French monk Bernard who saw it in 870 AD. Bernard was a Breton monk from the monastery of Mont St.-Michel. He was also known as Bernardus Francus, Bernardus Sapiens (Bernard the Wise), and Bernardus Monachus (Bernard the Monk; Monachus is derived from the 4th century Byzantine Greek μοναχός, monk, via the post classical Latin *monachus*, monk). In his journal Bernard recalls, "I must not, however, omit to state, that on Holy Saturday, which is the eve of Easter, the office is begun in the morning in this church, and after it is ended the *Kyrie Eleison* is chanted, until an angel comes and lights the lamps which hang over the aforesaid sepulchre; of which light the patriarch gives their shares to the bishops and to the rest of the people, that each may illuminate his own house. The present patriarch is called Theodosius, and was brought to this place on account of his piety from his monastery, which is fifteen miles from Jerusalem, and was made patriarch over all the Christians in the Land of Promise."[1] Bernard's text was discovered by Jean Mabillon in a manuscript of the library at Rheims and printed in the *Acts of the Saints of the Order of St. Benedict* [*Acta sanctorum Ordinis Sancti Benedicti*, 9 vols. (Paris, 1668-1710)]. Mabillon's text indicates that the year of authorship is 870 AD. Bernard's departure from Europe is fixed at 867. Theodosius was the Patriarch of Jerusalem from 863-879.

In modern times thousands of pilgrims travel to Jerusalem from all over the world and sit faithfully with unlit candles outside the tomb of Christ on Holy Saturday (according to the Julian calendar). In some eyewitness accounts, a flash of light descends and remains over the tomb. On some years, the unlit candles of the pilgrims who are seated outside the tomb miraculously light by themselves at the moment when the Patriarch's candle lights. Timothy Ware, in *The Orthodox Church*, chronicles an early 12th century account of this annual miracle: "A Russian pilgrim at Jerusalem in 1106-7, Abbot Daniel of Tchernigov, found Greeks and Latins worshipping together in harmony at the Holy Places, though he noted with satisfaction that at the ceremony of the Holy Fire the Greek lamps were lit miraculously while the Latin had to be lit from the Greek.[2] It is a historical fact that the candle does not miraculously light for the Vatican or Anglican envoys when they pass their candles over the Holy Sepulcher, but rather, they have to turn and receive their light from an Orthodox priest.

Let us examine Abbot Daniel's account of the Holy Flame. In his narrative of 1107 AD, the Russian Orthodox monk declares:

> The following is a description of the Holy Light, which descends upon the Holy Sepulchre, as the Lord vouchsafed to show it to me, his wicked and unworthy servant. For in very truth I have seen with my own sinful eyes how that Holy Light descends upon the redeeming Tomb of our Lord Jesus Christ. Many pilgrims relate incorrectly the details about the descent of that Holy Light. Some say that the Holy Ghost descends upon the Holy Sepulchre in the form of a dove; others that it is lightning from heaven which kindles the lamps above the Sepulchre of the Lord. This is all untrue, for neither dove nor lightning is to be seen at that moment; but the Divine grace comes down unseen from heaven, and lights the lamps of the Sepulchre of our Lord. I will only describe it in perfect truth as I have seen it. On Holy Friday, after Vespers, they clean the Holy Sepulchre and wash all the lamps that are there; they fill the lamps with pure oil without water and after having put in the wicks, leave them unlighted they affix the seals to the Tomb at the second hour of the night. At the same time they extinguish all the lamps and wax candles in every church in Jerusalem. Upon that same Friday, at the first hour of the day, I, the unworthy, entered the presence of Prince

Baldwin, and bowed myself to the ground before him. Seeing me, as I bowed, he bade me, in a friendly manner, come to him, and said, "What dost thou want, Russian abbot?" for he knew me and like me, being a man of great kindness and humility and not given to pride. I said to him, "My prince...allow me to place my lamp on the Holy Sepulchre in the name of the whole Russian country." Then with peculiar kindness and attention he gave me permission to place my lamp on the Sepulchre of the Lord, and sent one of his chief retainers with me to the custodian of the Resurrection, and to the keeper of the keys of the Holy Sepulchre. The custodian and the keeper of the keys directed me to bring my lamp filled with oil. I thanked them, and hastened, with much joy, to purchase a very large glass lamp; having filled it with pure oil, I carried it to the Holy Sepulchre towards evening, and was conducted to the afore-mentioned keeper, who was alone in the chapel of the Tomb. Opening the sacred portal for me, he ordered me to take off my shoes; and then having admitted me barefooted to the Holy Sepulchre, with the lamp that I bore, he directed me to place it on the Tomb of the Lord. I placed it, with my sinful hands, on the spot occupied by the sacred feet of our Lord Jesus Christ; the lamp of the Greeks being where the head lay, and that of St. Sabbas and all the monasteries in the position of the breast; for it is the custom of the Greeks and of the Monastery of St. Sabbas to place their lamps there each year. By God's grace these three lamps kindled on that occasion, but not one of those belonging to the Franks, which hung above, received the light. After having placed my lamp on the Holy Sepulchre, and after having adored and kissed, with penitence and pious tears, the sacred place upon which the body of our Lord Jesus Christ lay; I left the Holy Tomb filled with joy, and retired to my cell...

At the end of the ninth hour, when they commenced chanting the Canticle of the passage (of the Red Sea), "Cantabo Domino," a small cloud, coming suddenly from the east, rested above the open dome of the church; fine rain fell on the Holy Sepulchre, and wet us and all those who were above the Tomb. It was at this moment that the Holy Light suddenly illuminated the Holy Sepulchre, shining with an awe-aspiring and splendid brightness. The bishop, who was followed by four deacons, then opened the doors of the Tomb, and entered with the taper of Prince Baldwin so as to light it first at the Holy Light; he afterwards returned it to the Prince, who resumed his place, holding, with great joy, the taper in his hands. We lighted our tapers from that of the Prince, and so passed on the flame to everyone in the church.

This Holy Light is like no ordinary flame, for it burns in a marvellous way with indescribable brightness, and a ruddy colour like that of cinnabar. All the people remain standing with lighted tapers, and repeat in a loud voice with intense joy and eagerness: "Lord, have mercy upon us!" Man can experience no joy like that which every Christian feels at the moment when he sees the Holy Light of God. He who has not taken part in the glory of that day will not believe the record of all that I have seen. It is only wise, believing men who will place complete trust in the truth of this narrative, and who will hear with delight all the details concerning the holy places. He who is faithful in little will also be faithful in much; but to the wicked and incredulous the truth seems always a lie. God and the Holy Sepulchre of our Lord bear witness to my stories and to my humble person; so do my companions from Russia, Novgorod, and Kief: Iziaslav Ivanovitch, Gorodislav Mikhailovitch, the two Kashkitch, and many others who were there the same day.

But to return to my narrative. Directly the light shone in the Holy Sepulchre, the chant ceased, and all, crying out "Kyrie Eleison," moved towards the church with great joy, bearing the lighted tapers in their hands, and protecting them from the wind. Everyone then goes home; and the people after lighting the lamps of the churches with their tapers, remain in them to terminate the Vespers; whilst the priests alone, and without assistance, finish the Vespers in the great Church of the Holy Sepulchre. Carrying the lighted tapers, we returned to our monastery with the abbot and the monks; we finished the Vespers there and then retired to our cells, praising God for having condescended to show us unworthy ones His Divine grace. The morning of Holy Sunday…the abbot, cross in hand, and all monks singing the hymn, "Immortal One, Thou hast deigned to go down into the Tomb." Having entered the Holy Sepulchre, we covered the life-giving tomb of the Lord with kisses and scorching tears; we breathed with ecstasy the perfume which the presence of the Holy Ghost had left; and we gazed in admiration on the lamps which still burned with a bright and marvelous splendour. The custodian and the keeper of the keys told us, and the abbot, that the three lamps had kindled. The five other lamps suspended above were also burning, but their light was different from that of the three first, and had not that marvelous brightness. We afterwards left the tomb by the west door, and having proceeded to the high altar, kissed the Orthodox and received absolution; we then, with the abbot and the monks, left the Temple of the Holy Resurrection, and returned to our monastery to rest until it was time for mass.

The third day after the Resurrection of our Lord I went, after mass, to the keeper of the keys of the Holy Sepulchre, and said, "I wish to take away my lamp." He received me kindly, and made me enter the Tomb quite alone. I saw my lamp on the Holy Sepulchre still burning with the flame of that holy light; I prostrated myself before the sacred Tomb, and, with penitence, covered the sacred place where the pure body of our Lord Jesus Christ lay with kisses and tears. I afterwards measured the length, width, and height of the Tomb as it now is a thing which no one can do before witnesses. I gave (the keeper of the keys) of the Tomb of the Lord as much as I could, and offered him, according to my means, a small, poor gift. The keeper of the keys, seeing my love for the Holy Sepulchre, pushed back the slab that covers the part of the sacred Tomb on which Christ's head lay, and broke off a morsel of the sacred rock; this he gave me as a blessed memorial, begging me at the same time not to say anything about it at Jerusalem. After again kissing the Tomb of the Lord, and greeting the keeper, I took up my lamp, filled with holy oil, and left the Holy Sepuchre full of joy, enriched by the Divine grace, and bearing in my hand a gift from the sacred place, and a token from the Holy Sepulchre of our Lord. I went on my way rejoicing as if I were the bearer of vast wealth, and returned to my cell full of great joy.[3]

Having witnessed the descent of the Holy Flame in the Church of the Resurrection on Easter Sunday 1107 AD, and having procured a precious piece of rock cut off from the Lord's Tomb, Abbot Daniel began his journey home to Russia.

In modern times thousands of pilgrims continue to travel to Jerusalem each year to witness the Miracle of the Holy Flame. Many Internet websites describe the miracle and provide eyewitness testimonies of some of these pilgrims.[4] One website summarizes the miracle thus:

At a certain moment the Holy Light flashes from the depth of the Holy Sepulchre in a supernatural way, miraculously, and lights up the little lamp of olive oil put on the edge of it…

The Holy Light is not only distributed by the Archbishop, but operates also by itself. It emits from the Holy Sepulchre having a gleam of a hue completely different from that on natural light. It sparkles, it flashes like lightning. It flies like a dove around the tabernacle of the Holy Sepulchre, and lights up the unlit lamps of olive oil hanging in front if it. It whirls from one side of the church to the other. It enters into some of the chapels inside the church, as for instance the chapel of the Calvary (at a higher level than the Holy Sepulchre) and lights up the little lamps. It lights up also the candles of certain pilgrims. In fact there are some very pious pilgrims who, every time they attended this ceremony, noticed that their candles lit up on the own accord!

…As soon as it appears it has a bluish hue and does not burn. At the first moments of its appearance, if it touches the face, or the mouth, or the hands, it does not burn. This is proof of its divine and supernatural origin.[5]

Prof. Niels Christian Hvidt has traveled to the Church of the Resurrection and provides the following eyewitness account in his Internet article:

In order to find out, I traveled to Jerusalem to be present at the ceremony in which the Miracle of the Holy Fire occurs, and I can testify that it did not only happen in the ancient Church and throughout the Middle Ages but also on the 18th of April, 1998. The Greek-Orthodox

Patriarch of Jerusalem, Diodorus I, is the man who every
year enters the tomb to receive the Holy Fire…

…the Israeli authorities on this Easter Saturday come
and seal the tomb with wax. Before they seal the door it
is customary that they enter the tomb to check for any
hidden source of fire, which could produce the miracle
through fraud. Just as the Romans were to guarantee
that there was no manipulation after the death of Jesus,
likewise the Israeli Local Authorities are to guarantee
that there be no trickery in 1998…[6]

Hvidt procured an interview with His Beatitude, Diodorus I,
the Patriarch of Jerusalem, who described his experience inside
the tomb of the Lord. This is what how the Patriarch, who
experiences the miracle every year, describes it:

"From the core of the very stone on which Jesus lay an
indefinable light pours forth. It usually has a blue tint,
but the color may change and take many different hues.
It cannot be described in human terms. The light rises
out of the stone as mist may rise out of a lake. It almost
looks as if the stone is covered by a moist cloud, but it is
light. This light each year behaves differently. Sometimes
it covers just the stone, while other times it gives light to
the whole sepulchre, so that people who stand outside
the tomb and look into it will see it filled with light. The
light does not burn. I have never had my beard burnt in
all the sixteen years I have been Patriarch in Jerusalem
and have received the Holy Fire. The light is of a different
consistency than normal fire that burns in an oil lamp.

At a certain point the light rises and forms a column in
which the fire is of a different nature, so that I am able to
light my candles from it. When I thus have received the

flame on my candles, I go out and give the fire first to the Armenian Patriarch and then to the Coptic. Hereafter I give the flame to all people present in the Church...

For me personally it is of great comfort to consider Christ's faithfulness towards us, which he displays by giving us the holy flame every year in spite of our human frailties and failures. We experience many wonders in our Churches, and miracles are nothing strange to us. It happens often that icons cry, when Heaven wants to display its closeness to us...["]7

Mr. Hvidt concludes:

The miracle is not confined to what actually happens inside the little tomb, where the Patriarch prays. What may be even more significant, is that the blue light is reported to appear and be active outside the tomb. Every year many believers claim that this miraculous light ignites candles, which they hold in their hands, of its own initiative. All in the church wait with candles in the hope that they may ignite spontaneously. Often closed oil lamps take fire by themselves before the eyes of the pilgrims. The blue flame is seen to move in different places in the Church. A number of signed testimonies by pilgrims, whose candles lit spontaneously, attest to the validity of these ignitions.[8]

Endnotes

1   Bernard, *The Voyage of Bernard the Wise, A.D. 867* in *Early Travels in Palestine, comprising the Narratives of Arculf, Willibald, Bernard, Sæwulf, Sigurd, Benjamin of Tudela, Sir John Maundeville, De La Brocquière, and Maundrell,* edited and annotated by Thomas Wright (London: Henry G. Bohn, 1848), 27.

2   Timothy Ware, *The Orthodox Church,* revised edition (London: Penguin Books, 1997), 59.

3   Abbot Daniel of Tchernigov, *The Pilgrimage of the Russian Abbot Daniel in the Holy Land 1106-1107 AD,* translated from the French by Madame Sophie de Khitrowo, edited by C.W. Wilson (London: Palestine Pilgrims' Text Society, 1895), 74-75, 78-81.

4   A plethora of websites can be procured by triangulating "Holy Flame" and "Orthodox Church" on your search engine. Below are some websites. Note that some addresses are case sensitive: http://www.ocf.org/OrthodoxPage/reading/light.html (Mar. 22, 2007), www.orthodoxinfo.com/general/holyfire.asp (Mar. 22, 2007), www.holyfire.org/eng/doc_MiracleEncounters.htm (Mar. 22, 2007), www2.cytanet.com.cy/gogreek/miracle.htm (Mar. 22, 2007)

5   http://www.ocf.org/OrthodoxPage/reading/light.html (Mar. 22, 2007)

6   www.orthodoxinfo.com/general/holyfire.asp (Mar. 22, 2007)

7   Ibid.

8   Ibid.

CHAPTER SIX

Miracles Performed by the Saints

...I looked in his face and there came over me an even greater reverential awe. Imagine the centre of the sun, in the dazzling brilliance of his midday rays, the face of the man who talks with you. You see the movement of his lips and the changing expression of his eyes, you hear his voice, you feel someone grasp your shoulders; yet you do not see the hands, you do not even see yourself or his figure, but only a blinding light spreading several yards around and throwing a sparkling radiance across the snow blanket...
—**Nicholas Motovilov,** *A Conversation of St. Seraphim of Sarov with Nicholas Motovilov concerning the Aim of the Christian Life* **(1831)**

THE MIRACLES THAT ARCHANGEL MICHAEL PERFORMED AT CHAIROTOPA AND COLOSSAE IN THE MID-FIRST CENTURY AD

The glory of God's creation is attested to by all of His creatures, by humans on earth and by His angels in Heaven, as well. The Archangel Michael is one of the principal angels in Heaven and he is mentioned several times in the Bible. Whenever he is, he is portrayed not only as God's servant, but also as God's warrior whom God sends when special strength is needed to fight the principalities of darkness. Michael is mentioned five times in the Bible: in Dan 10:13, Dan 10:21, Dan 12:1, Jude 9, and Rev 12:7.

In the first instance, Michael is referred to as one of the chief princes who fought alongside the archangel Gabriel to overturn the Persian monarchies: "But the prince of the kingdom of Persia withstood me one and twenty days: but, lo, Michael, one of the chief princes, came to help me; and I remained there with the kings of Persia" (Dan 10:13). Here Gabriel is telling Daniel that he and Michael have been engaged in a battle. From the text we must necessarily extrapolate that the battle that Gabriel is relating is a spiritual battle: "The prince of the kingdom of Persia" withstood the power of the Archangel Gabriel, and so, we know that this prince must be more than a man, he must be an angelic being. Furthermore, he must be an evil angel because he opposed Gabriel and Michael, who are angels of God.

The battle that Gabriel and Michael fought together against the principalities of darkness lasted for 21 days, the exact period of time that Daniel had been fasting and praying in Dan 10:2. This agreement in time between Daniels' three weeks of self-denial (Dan 10:2) and the three week battle between the good angels and the prince of the kingdom of Persia (Dan 10:13) indicates that the two events are connected. Victory came on the 21st day because Daniel remained in mourning for a full three weeks.

There are a few lessons to be learned here. First, the phrase, "Michael, one of the chief princes, came to help me" in Dan 10:13 indicates that Michael is a servant of God who engages in spiritual battles on behalf of the Lord. He is mentioned again in Dan 10:21: "No one supports me against them except Michael" (NIV). Again, Archangels Gabriel and Michael fight battles on behalf of God in the spiritual realm. This indicates that a correlation exists between earthly kingdoms and spiritual realms. Persia was governed by an evil entity who was so powerful that Gabriel and Michael together were needed to defeat him: "But the prince of the kingdom of Persia withstood me one and twenty days" (Dan 10:13). We know that only an angelic entity could withstand the strength of Gabriel and Michael combined. We also know that this being's stance against two angels of the Lord indicates that he is evil in nature. Therefore, the text is teaching us that earthly kingdoms are governed by good or evil spiritual kingdoms. Persia, a seat of pagan idolatry, was governed by the principalities of darkness. It was Daniel's continual and steadfast fasting and prayer for 21 days in the physical realm, occurring concurrently with Gabriel and Michael's spiritual battle against the demon that ruled Persia in the spiritual realm, that caused the kingdoms of Persia to fall. Kings and world leaders can give themselves over to good or evil realms. The fruit they bear is the telltale sign as to whom their allegiance is pledged.

Furthermore, we learn from this historical account of the fall of Persia that persistence in prayer is important. It is because Daniel fasted and prayed for 21 days that his prayers were answered and the Kingdom of Persia fell. God's desire that his people pray continuously is taught by Christ in Luke 11:5-8.

Michael is mentioned again in Dan 12:1. This verse prophecizes about end times and the rise of the Antichrist: "And at that time shall Michael stand up, the great prince which standeth for the children of thy people: and there shall be a time of trouble, such as never was since there was a nation even to that same time: and at that time thy people shall be delivered, every one that shall be found written in the book" (Dan 12:1). This "time of trouble" is reiterated as the time of Jacob's trouble in Jer 30:7, by Christ in Mat 24:21, by John in Rev 16:8, and discussed in great detail in Rev 6-18.

Michael appears again in Revelation: "And there was war in heaven: Michael and his angels fought against the dragon; and the dragon fought and his angels, And prevailed not; neither was their place found any more in heaven: (Rev 12:7-8). This is a prophecy of end times when the Archangel Michael will defeat the principalities of darkness again. Until this event occurs, evil angels are permitted access to Heaven in order to accuse God's servants on earth (Job 1:6-11; 2:1-5). When Michael and his angels are finally permitted to engage the evil angels in Heaven, they cast them to earth where they can no longer accuse God's people. Again we see Michael as a powerful warrior angel battling and conquering the forces of evil in the spiritual realm. Again, Rev 12, like Dan 10, point out that spiritual battles in the heavenly realms correspond with events taking place on earth.

This prefatory examination of biblical verses that mention Michael provides an understanding of his role as protector of humankind. Rebellious angels declare war on humanity in the spiritual realm and this has repercussions in the physical realm. Michael is ever ready to fight them to stem paganism on earth.

In addition to protecting humans from demonic influences in the spiritual realm, there is also biblical evidence that angels take part in healing people of diseases. John 5:4 says, "For an angel went down at a certain season into the pool, and troubled the water: whosoever then first after the troubling of the water stepped in was made whole of whatsoever disease he had." Although the Bible does not provide the name of the angel who agitated the water in the pool of Bethesda, the verse does reveal that in biblical times God provided healing in miraculous pools via His angels.

There is physical evidence, both textual and geographic, that during the Church Age, the Archangel Michael has performed numerous miracles of healing (sometimes creating springs and rerouting rivers via an earthquake). One early miracle occurred during the middle of the first century at Chairotopa (present day Ceretapa, Turkey) when Michael intervened in human affairs and created a miraculous spring of healing. There are three Greeks texts, a Latin recension (revision), and an Ethiopian text that attest to this miracle.

In the Greek account of the miracle, the apostles John and Philip traveled through Chairotopa and announced to the villagers that the Archangel Michael would soon perform a miracle for them. As soon as the apostles departed from the city, Michael caused a spring to gush forth that had miraculous curative powers. Soon Chairotopa was renown for its miraculous healing spring and sick people from all over Asia Minor made pilgrimages to the site seeking cures for their diseases. In once instance, a pagan from Laodicea had a daughter who had been born mute. Michael appeared to the man in a vision and advised him that if his daughter were to go to the spring and drink from it, her speech would be restored. The man journeyed to Chairotopa from Laodicea and when his daughter drank from the spring, she was miraculously healed. The man and his entire family became Christians and were baptized. In gratitude the man built a chapel to St. Michael at the site of the holy spring.

Many years later, the pagan population residing in Chairotopa plotted to destroy both St. Michael's church sanctuary and the spring. They dug several canals in an attempt to divert two rivers running from a mountain towards the shrine to flood it. However, a monk named Archippos, who had taken residency in the sanctuary, prayed to St. Michael to save the shrine and the spring. By the sign of the Cross and a massive earthquake, St. Michael opened a deep fissure in the ground at Colossae and caused the path of the two rivers to funnel into an underground course, thus saving both the sanctuary and the spring. Colossae, the site of the earthquake, lies 30 miles northwest of Chairotopa in the mountains of present day southwestern Turkey, near Denizli. Because of this miracle, the name of Colossae was changed to Chonae, which means "funnels" in Greek. Today Chonae is Khonas, Turkey and is situated on the Lycus River. Hence, two distinct and separate geographical phenomena have occurred as a result of St. Michael's intervention: the first is the creation of the miraculous spring at Chairotopa; the second is the funneling of the rivers that occurred at Colossae. The Feast Day of the Archangel Michael, held by the Orthodox on September 6, commemorates these great miracles.

In addition, the hot springs in Pythia in Bithynia have been dedicated to Michael as a result of their curative powers; he established miraculous healing waters at the ancient site of Germia (Yürme, Turkey); a sanctuary dedicated to him, the Michaelion, was built at Sosthenion, fifty miles from Constantinople, after he appeared to Constantine there; a church was built for him in Constantinople at the thermal baths of the Emperor Arcadius (the Thermae of Arcadius); in Egypt Christians place the Nile under the protection of St. Michael.

MIRACLES PERFORMED BY SAINT HARALAMBOS C. 193 AD

Saint Haralambos was ordained as a priest at a very early age and then became the Bishop of Magnesia (now Manisa, near the western coast of Turkey). He lived a very long life and when he reached the age of 107, he was tortured and martyred for his faith in Christ. For this reason he is called a hieromartyr, which in the Greek calendar designates a martyr who had holy orders. In Greek ιερέας means priest, minister, vicar; μάρτυρας, witness or martyr. Hence, a hieromartyr is a martyr who has received holy orders (is ordained as a priest).

Saint Haralambos lived in the second century during the reign of the pagan Roman Emperor Septimius Serverus (who ruled 193-211 AD). Haralambos stood in opposition to the pagan religion of the Roman Empire and vociferously instructed the inhabitants of his community that Christ is the Way, the Truth, and the Life, and the only path to the One True God. It was for this reason that he was brought before the tribunal of the Roman Governor in charge of Asia Minor, Lucian. Lucian had Haralambos submitted to an endless litany of horrific tortures that would have most certainly killed him if it had not been for divine intervention.

First Lucian had Haralamabos submitted to a process by which iron claws tore into and lacerated his flesh. However, the elderly bishop of Magnesia never cried out in pain and ended by thanking his torturers for mortifying his flesh, renewing his soul, and hence, preparing him to enter the Kingdom of the One True God, Jesus Christ.

When the Roman Governor Lucian saw that he was unable to effect Haralambos' conversion to paganism via torture, he became enraged and lunged at him uncontrollably, tearing at his flesh with his bare hands. At this point, God intervened and performed a miracle: Lucian's arms became severed from his body at the elbows and his hands remained clawed on his victim's body. Lucian cried out in horror and begged Haralambos for mercy. The saint prayed to the Lord to forgive him his sins and heal him and God granted his request. When Lucian was miraculously healed and his hands were restored, he was astounded by two things: his own miraculous dismemberment and subsequent healing, and the surprising virtue of Christians to forgive their enemies, a quality unknown to pagans. As a result, the Roman Governor Lucian, the two torturers, Porphyrius and Baptus, and three pagan women who were onlookers, all believed in Christ and were baptized. The news of the miracle spread throughout Asia Minor and many pagans converted to Christianity and were baptized.

As the inhabitants of Magnesia began converting to Christianity and God was being glorified, many more miracles started to happen: the blind saw for the first time, the crippled began to walk. These miracles occurred when Haralambos prayed over the sick.

The Emperor of Rome, Septimius Severus, was a pagan zealot and when he heard that the inhabitants of Magnesia were converting to Christianity en masse because of Haralambos, he decided that the elderly bishop must be tortured mercilessly and then be put to death. Keep n mind that Haralambos was 107 years old at the time: the unspeakable torture to which he was about to be submitted would be horrific enough for a younger man, let alone a very thin, frail centenarian.

Severus sent 300 soldiers to Magnesia to seize the bishop and bring him to Antioch where Severus was residing at the time. The soldiers arrested Haralambos and then mistreated him badly en route to Antioch. Then another miracle happened: the horse on which Haralambos rode began to speak, declaring that the Emperor Severus was the enemy of God, as were the soldiers themselves. The soldiers became terrified and left Haralambos alone for the remainder of the journey.

When Haralambos arrived in Antioch, the Emperor Severus submitted him to a series of hideous, brutal assaults. First he ordered that he be pierced with a skewer and thrown into a blazing furnace. However, the skewer did not kill the saint, the fire did not burn his skin, and in fact, the flames self-extinguished the moment they touched his body.

Next Severus presented Haralambos with a demoniac who had been possessed for 35 years. The saint exorcized the demon from the man and healed him.

Then Severus presented Haralambos with the corpse of a young man laying in his casket. The saint took the man's hand and the man sat up in his bier as if awakening from sleep.

Severus ordered Haralambos to sacrifice to idols. The Christian bishop refused and Severus ordered his men to break his jaws with stones and set his beard on fire. At this point God intervened and performed a series of astounding miracles: the flames directed themselves towards the assailants and a great earthquake shook the ground on which they stood. Then Emperor Severus was lifted up from his throne, suspended in midair, and thrashed for a long time by angels. Severus had a daughter, Galinia, and when she heard of these happenings, she believed in Christ and confessed that He is Lord. She asked Haralambos to pray to God to forgive her father his sins and release him from the punishment that he was suffering.

Haralambos asked God to release Severus from his ordeal and God granted his prayer. However, Severus was not grateful and gave orders to have Haralambos tortured some more. He also threatened his daughter with death unless she abandon Christianity and sacrifice to the idols. Galinia entered the temple and smashed all the statues into pieces. Severus had new statues made, but as soon as they were installed in the temple, she smashed these, too.

At this point Severus ordered that Haralambos be executed. When Haralambos was delivered to the place where his execution would take place, he raised his arms towards the sky and thanked God for the privilege of being martyred for Christ. A voice came forth from the heavens above which everyone present heard. The voice invited him to enter Heaven and share his place with the martyrs and holy priests. Then he was beheaded by the sword. His body was buried by St. Galinia. Today his skull rests at the Monastery of St. Stephen in Meteora (in northern Greece). Fragments of his relics are kept throughout Greece and elsewhere in the world and have performed many miracles down through the centuries. His feast day is February 10, the day of his execution.

MIRACLES PERFORMED BY SAINT THEODORE THE TYRON C. 303 AD

Historians do not agree as to why St. Theodore was called "the Tyron." According to some, it is because during the time of the Roman Empire, "tyron" meant young soldier or recruit. It is derived from the ancient Latin *tīro*, in med. Latin spelled *tyro*, meaning a young soldier, recruit, beginner. Today the word means simply a beginner, learner or novice. According to others, he is called "the Tyron" because for a time he belonged to the *Cohors Tyronum*. In Roman antiquity a *cohors* was a body of infantry in the Roman army of which there were ten in a legion, each consisting of 300-600 men. Therefore, a *cohors* was a company of soldiers, a tenth part of a legion. For a time he belonged to the Legion of Tyre, a coastal city of what is today Lebanon.

Theodore came from Amasia (today Amasya, Turkey) in the Pontic Mountains not far from the Black Sea. He belonged to the Roman legion at the time of Maximian's persecution of Christians. Theodore, devout in his allegiance to Christ, was vocal in his opposition to pagan rituals. One day the commander of the Roman army, Brincus, ordered him to offer sacrifice to the gods of the Empire. Theodore refused and informed his squad commander that he was a Christian and that he worshipped Christ alone. That night he went to the altar of Rhea, the mother of the gods, and destroyed it. He was caught in the act and brought before the governor Publius. The governor ordered that he be thrown into prison and starved. Christ appeared to Theodore while he was in prison and promised him that his grace would be his food and drink, joy and shield. Theodore, although alone in his cell, sang hymns with angels who were present, and the jailors heard numerous voices singing in harmony and thought that there were other Christians in the cell with him.

The next day he was presented to Publius a second time and offered the post of high priest of the idols. Theodore refused and as punishment, was hung by heels and his body was lacerated with iron claws. During the torture Theodore remained silent and did not cry out in pain. When the torture was completed, he was condemned to be burned at the stake.

When Theodore arrived at the stake, he jumped upon the pyre and walked freely through the flames; the fire did not burn him. Then, in the midst of the circle of flames, Theodore voluntarily surrendered his soul to God; however, his body remained unburned. The Christian princess Eusebia took possession of his body and returned him to Euchaïta (today Beyözü, in central Turkey), where a church was built in honor of him. After his death, the martyr performed many miracles of healing there for pilgrims who came asking for help.

In addition, Theodore is recognized as having performed a special miracle to prevent Christians residing in Constantinople from eating food that had been sacrificed to idols. In 361 AD Julian the Apostate tried to restore pagan ritual to the city. He ordered that all of the food sold in the market place be sprinkled with the blood of sacrificed animals so that no one would escape eating food that was the product of pagan idolatry. However, God sent His servant Thedodore to appear in a vision to Patriarch Eudoxius of Constantinople some time during the years 360-364 to warn him. In the vision Theodore explained to the Patriarch what was happening and told him to instruct Christians not to buy food from the market, but rather, to eat *kolyva* (made from grains of boiled wheat, sugar or honey, fruit and/or nuts). Hence, Theodore is credited with having prevented Christendom from committing the sin of eating food that had been sacrificed to idols. The Orthodox Church commemorates the appearance of Theodore to Patriarch Eudoxius and his instruction to eat *kolyva* on the first Saturday of Lent. This is done to remind Christians that fasting and temperance are keys to avoiding sin. The faithful bring *kolyva* to church in memory of family and friends who have died in Christ.

Theodore also performed many other miracles after his martyrdom. He is credited with appearing in a vision to a widow whose only son had been captured by the Saracens. In the vision the glorified Theodore who had attained theosis sat on his white horse; shortly afterwards the widow's son escaped from capture and returned home unharmed. St. Theodore has also brought to safety those caught in storms at sea and has revealed the identity of thieves to their victims. Theodore has come to be regarded as the protector of Christians.

MARY'S MIRACLE IN CONSTANTINOPLE IN 626 AD

In 626 AD Persia attacked the Byzantine Empire. This was the worst possible time for Byzantium to get attacked because its emperor, Heraclius, was away on an expedition to fight the aggression of the Persians on their own grounds. In the absence of the Emperor, barbaric hordes of Avars (a Turkic people prominent in south-eastern Europe during the 6th-9th centuries AD) approached the walls of Constantinople, surrounded the city, and proceeded to lay siege to it. The siege continued for a few months. The Avars enjoyed two advantages: they outnumbered the Byzantines and, because they surrounded the city, the Byzantines could not introduce more armies into the city to fight.

The Patriarch of Constantinople, Sergius I (Patriarch from 610 until he died, on December 9, 638) and the High Official Vonos, asked Mary, the Mother of Christ, for help. Holding a holy icon of Mary, they marched around the periphery of the walls of Constantinople and sang praises to the Mother of God. After the procession a great miracle occurred: a huge storm with crushing tidal waves came and destroyed most of the enemy's invading fleet and saved the city. Weakened by this disaster, the Avars fully retreated.

After this miracle, Christians gathered into the Church of the Theotokos at Vlachernae on the Golden Horn. The Patriarch celebrated the liturgy and the faithful stood all night, singing thanks and praise to Mary for her assistance. The hymn that they sung has come to be called the Akathist Hymn, from the Greek *akathistos*, not seated. The hymn is also known as the "Laudations or Salutations [*Heretismoi*] to the Theotokos."

The Akathist Hymn has become an integral part of Orthodox liturgy and is chanted in all Orthodox churches during the weeks preceding Holy Week. Comprised of 24 stanzas that alternate between short and long, it is divided into four parts. One part is sung on each Friday of Lent. A part is performed on the first Friday of Lent and another part is sung on each subsequent Friday until two Fridays before Good Friday for a total of five times. On the fifth Friday, the entire hymn is sung in commemoration of the miracle that Mary performed in Constantinople in 626 AD. It is believed that the Akathist Hymn was written by St. Romanos the Melodist in Constantinople; however, since then it has evolved into a composite work of several hymnographers.

MIRACLES THAT ST. MACARIOS NOTARAS OF CORINTH PERFORMED AFTER HIS DEATH

St. Macarios Notaras of Corinth (1731-1805), named Michael by his parents, was ordained the Archbishop of Corinth in January 1765. St. Macarios is best known for his book, the *Philokalia*, an anthology on asceticism, solitude, and prayer of the heart (hesychasm), compiled from thirty-eight fathers of the Church and published in 1782. St. Macarios was co-editor of this work with St. Nicodemus Hagiorita of Mount Athos (1749-1809).

Constantine Cavarnos provides a biography of the saint in his work entitled, *St. Macarios of Corinth: Archbishop of Corinth, Guardian of Sacred Tradition, Reviver of Orthodox Mysticism, Compiler of the Philokalia, Spiritual Striver, Enlightener and Guide, and Trainer of Martyrs: An Account of His Life, Character and Message, Together with Selections from Three of His Publications.*[1] In this study Cavarnos includes an account of the miracles that the relics of St. Macarios performed, as described by the saint's close friend Athanasios Parios in his work, entitled, *Akoluthia of Our Father Saint Macarios Notaras, Archbishop of Corinth [Akolouthia tou en hagiois Patros hemon Makariou, Archiepiskopou Korinthou tou*

Notara].[2] It is fortunate that Cavarnos has translated the accounts from Parios' Greek text for the English-speaking world.

The historicity of these miracles is substantiated by the names, places, and dates that Parios provides in his biography and that Cavarnos reiterates in his work. The inclusion of the names of doctors and surgeons, and the hospitals and cities in which they practiced, renders credible witness to Parios' testimony. Briefly, the miracles are as follows:

1. Argyri, a 4 year old girl, was dying of smallpox in Chios. Her mother, Angerou, and father, Frangoulis, sought help from Domenikos, the most highly regarded surgeon in all of Chios. In an effort to heal his patient, the surgeon removed not only the smallpox sores from her hand, but the bones beneath them, as well. After surgery the little girl's hand was rendered immobile and remained on a sling, with bones removed. The fact that a surgeon would actually removes bones from a patient dying of smallpox reminds us of how primitive the science of medicine was at the turn of the nineteenth century. However, then a great miracle of healing occurred: when Macarios died, the mother took her daughter, along with her niece, to the funeral to pay their respects to the holy man. Having arrived at the church, the mother venerated his body and prayed to him. It was not until they returned home that the mother discovered that her daughter had recovered from her illness and was able to move her arm without difficulty. When Doctor Domenikos removed her bandages, he was astounded to discover that her sores had healed. All of Chios, including both the religious and medical communities, recognized this as a miracle and Macarios gained renown as a healer.[3]

2. A tailor by the name of Nicholas Paraskevas, living in Upper Kyriaki, was dying of dropsy. Dropsy is a disease in which fluid accumulates in the serous cavities or the connective tissue of the body. Because the body is filled with water, the disease is characterized by swelling. The most experienced doctor in the city, Marinos Klados, was unable to help Nicholas and his condition worsened: his body became distended and he was at the point of death. However, Father Nikephoros had a piece of St. Macarios' relics which had previously worked many miracles on the sick and dying. Father Nikephoros visited the dying man, blessed him with St. Macarios' relic, crossed his body with holy water, and left. The sick man immediately recovered and was able to attend church the following day.[4]

3. Tryphon Hatjipsaras had a child who had a polyp on his palate. The boy's ailment was characterized by a red nose and an issue of blood emanating from his mouth. Physicians administered burning salves in their efforts to help him, without success. Then the father remembered that Macarios had healed little Argyri, the girl discussed in miracle #1 above. The father decided to take his child to a liturgy that was being held at Macarios' hermitage. Afterwards, the priest crossed and touched the child with the relics of Macarios and the child was instantly cured.[5]

4. Loula, the daughter of the physician Almanachos, suffered from paralysis throughout her body. Because she could move neither her arms, nor her legs, she was carried to the tomb of St. Macarios and crossed with his relics. She went home and the following day, her family discovered that she was completely cured of her paralysis.[6]

MIRACLES PERFORMED BY
ST. NIKEPHOROS OF CHIOS

St. Nikephoros (1750-1821) was a monk, teacher, Christian scholar, and author of liturgical poetry and biographies of the saints and martyrs. Constantine Cavarnos has written a biography of him, entitled, *St. Nikephoros of Chios: Outstanding Writer of Liturgical Poetry and Lives of Saints, Educator, Spiritual Striver, and Trainer of Martyrs: An Account of His Life, Character and Message, Together with a Comprehensive List of His Publications, Selections from Them, and Brief Biographies of Eleven Neomartyrs and Other Orthodox Saints Who are Treated in His Works*.[7] In his biography Cavarnos includes an abridged translation of Emily Sarou's *The Life of St. Nikephoros* [*Bios tou Hosiou Nikephorou tou Chiou*].[8] Sarou cites many miracles of healing that St. Nikephoros peformed. Briefly, they are as follows:

1. A sick woman of Kallismasia sought St. Nikephoros hoping that he would heal her. When he met her, he touched her with a relic of St. Macarios that he always carried on his person, and instantly healed her.[9]
2. St. Nikephoros permanently cured a deranged girl who lived in Kallismasia.[10]
3. He also permanently healed a madman in Vrontados.[11]
4. He healed another man residing in Vrontados by the name of Nicholas Lodis. Mr. Lodis had a dream in which St. Nikephoros instructed him to go to his grave and procure some soil. This dream occurred just after the saint's relics had been removed from his grave and taken to another location. The morning after his dream, Mr. Lodis visited the saint's empty grave, took some soil, and then had a holy water ceremony performed [*hagiasmos*]. He was immediately cured of his illness.[12]
5. One day a thief stole St. Nikephoros' goat. However, the holy man did not harbor any ill feeling towards the

criminal: in fact, he told his disciple not to be angry because they had had the goat long enough and it was someone else's turn to benefit from it. The moment that he had spoken this, the thief presented himself and confessed his sin, saying that he was sorry that he slaughtered the goat. He also informed St. Nikephoros that he had found it impossible to sell the meat. The saint forgave him and told him that now he could sell the meat. When the thief returned home, his wife advised him that all of the meat had been sold.[13]

6. St. Nikephoros was known to be able to foresee and predict all suffering that would occur in the future.[14]

7. The monk Agathangelos of Hydra who lived in Resta saw the burial site of the saint in a dream in 1845. He had the site excavated and he found his sacred relics.[15]

SAINT HERMAN OF ALASKA

Most people do not know that Alaska is the only Orthodox state in the union. Beginning with the last decade of the eighteenth century and lasting throughout the nineteenth, Russian Orthodox missionaries have brought the Good News of the Risen Lord to the natives of Alaska, the Eskimos and the Aleuts. One such missionary was the tonsured monk St. Herman (c. 1756-1837).

On December 25, 1793 Herman left the Valaam Monastery in Russia, along with other monks, bound for Kodiak, Alaska. Their purpose was to bring Christianity to the natives of the newly discovered Aleutian Islands, a pagan people that had never heard of Christ. Finally, nine months later and after a journey of 7,000 miles, on September 24, 1793, they arrived in Kodiak. Their endless expedition marks the longest missionary journey in the history of the Orthodox Church. As a result of their labors, many thousands of Aleuts accepted Christ as their Lord and Savior and were baptized in the Orthodox faith.

Father Herman took residence on Spruce Island, which he called the New Valaam, after the monastery to which he had formally belonged, the famous Valaam Monastery on Lake Ladoga. When he first arrived on Spruce Island, he dug a cave in the ground with his bare hands and lived in it all summer. However, when winter arrived, the Russian American Company constructed a cell for him and he dwelt there during the remaining forty years of his life. The cave in the ground was to become his burial site.

The bittersweet biography of Herman transports us to another century, to the frigid temperatures of the high latitudes of Russia. It exposes us to self-abnegation and Spartan living conditions in undeveloped forests; to a deadly epidemic for which there was no cure that eviscerated entire villages; to the little orphans whom Herman fed and for whom he built a Christian school after they had lost their parents in the epidemic; to the unspeakable brutality of zealous Jesuits who cut off the fingers and toes, and then the arms and legs of an Orthodox Aleut, and forced him to bleed to death simply for declaring that he was already a Christian when pressed to convert to Roman Catholicism; to the documented miracles that Mary, the Mother of God, performed to save both him and the natives of Spruce Island from sickness, tidal waves, and fire.

Although Herman was never ordained a priest, the Aleuts called him "Father Herman" because he was the spiritual father of all. People came to him when they were in need and he always helped them. He founded a school for newly baptized children, as well as a church. He also ministered to the sick and dying at great personal risk at the time of an epidemic: in 1819 a ship from the United States brought a fatal epidemic, first to Sitka Island, and then to Kodiak Island. Entire families rapidly fell ill and died. The contagion was greatly facilitated by the fact that as many as a hundred Aleuts were housed in a single barracks, with people living in close proximity to one another, sleeping in adjacent bunks. The death toll was so high that for three days there was no one to bury the bodies. The sick and dying lay next to dead bodies; children whose parents had expired remained there, hungry and with no place to go. Herman selflessly ignored his own health and provided continual assistance to survivors and to the dying. He provided counsel, advised them to repent, and prepared them for death. He founded an orphanage for those who had lost their parents to the epidemic and provided for them, spiritually, as well as with food and shelter.

Another horrific incident was the martyrdom of Peter the Aleut. Yanovsky relates how he had told Herman about the forced conversions to Catholicism that the Spanish Jesuits were effecting in California. They gathered some Orthodox Aleuts and threatened them with torture if they would not convert. They responded to the Spaniards that they were already Christians. The Jesuits segregated them into pairs and cut off the fingers and toes of one while the other watched. Peter, whose last name has not been conserved, refused to convert. Then the Jesuits cut off his hands and feet and he died from blood loss. When Yanovsky related this account to Herman, the latter arose, lit a candle before an icon, and asked Peter the Aleut, a new holy martyr, to pray for them. Such was the brutality encountered by Orthodox Christians in California in the 19th century.

Research indicates that wherever there is persecution of the Church, there God pours forth miracles, and this was the case among Orthodox missionaries in America. Mary, the Mother of Christ, loved Herman, and she performed miracles for him on several occasions during his life when he was in dire need of help.

When Herman was 16 years old, he became a monk at the St. Sergius Hermitage in Russia. While he was residing there, he developed a carbuncle on the right side of his throat. A carbuncle is a multi-headed boil caused by a bacterial infection of the skin and subcutaneous tissue; abscess is usually discharged from more than one opening. Herman's carbuncle rapidly swelled and it became enlarged to the point that he had difficulty swallowing; a foul odor emanated from the site. Although it appeared that his life was in jeopardy, he did not consult a doctor. Rather, he retreated to his cell and prayed to Mary before her icon. Then he took a wet cloth, wiped it across the face of Mary on the icon, and placed the towel on his own face. He fell into a deep sleep and dreamt that Mary visited him and miraculously healed him. Indeed, when he awoke in the morning, he discovered that the abscess had disappeared, leaving only a small mark to remind him that a miracle had occurred.

Later in his life, when a tidal wave threatened Spruce Island, he placed an icon of the Virgin Mary on the beach and advised the natives that the flood would not come past the icon: Mary answered his prayer and the oncoming water stopped short of the icon. Today this icon can be seen on Spruce Island. On another occasion, a forest fire threatened the island and he dug a trench: the fire did not jump past the trench.

In addition, Herman received the gift of clairvoyance from God: he was able to predict the future and advise people, in an intensely personal way, of the challenges and obstacles that they would face in the future. Because the future is fluid or liquid and subject to change from moment to moment, Herman advised people what the general scenario would be and that they always had the choice of doing the right thing. Simeon Ivanovich Yanovsky, Governor of the Russian Colonies and disciple of Father Herman, documents that in one such case, Herman counseled a naval captain who had converted to Orthodoxy from Lutheranism by chrismation. When the naval captain was about to leave America, Herman warned him that if anything were to happen to his wife, that he must be extremely wary of whom he would then marry: his new wife could compromise his Orthodox faith. As it turned out, that is exactly what happened: his wife did die, he married someone who took him away from his faith, and he ended up dying suddenly without repentance. Did the naval captain have a choice? Yes, he did. He could have chosen not to marry her. Herman warned him: the rest was up to him.

Before Herman died, he made two predictions regarding his own death: first, that there would be no priest present to bury him and secondly, that he would be forgotten for 30 years. Both predictions came true. Although he died on November 15, 1837, there was no priest on the island to officiate at a funeral and so, he was not buried until December 13. In addition, he was forgotten for 30 years: it was not until 1867 that Bishop Peter of Alaska initiated an investigation into his life, sacrifices, and great contributions to the Kingdom of Christ.

One night a pillar of light, reaching from the ground up to the heavens, was seen in the village of Katari on Afognak Island. It turns out that that was the night that Father Herman had died. In addition, it was reported in another village on that same island that a figure of a man was seen rising up from the ground towards Heaven.

The information that we have of Father Herman originates from various primary sources. In 1864 a friend of Gerasim Ivanova-Zyrianov, Herman's disciple, brought news of Herman's life and work to the Abbot of the Valaam Monastery. The Abbot, intrigued by the account given by Gerasim's friend, wanted to know more. That year he sent letters of inquiry about Herman to the Hierarch Innocent, Archbishop of Kamchatka and the Aleutians, to Bishop Peter, the Vicar of the Kamchatka Diocese, and to Herman's disciple, Gerasim Zyrianov. It took three years for these inquiries to reach their destinations and for responses to return to the Abbot.

The following year, while the Abbot's letters were still in transit, the Governor of All Russian-American Colonies, Simeon Ivanovich Yanovsky, wrote to the Abbot of the Valaam Monastery. Yanovsky, who had formerly been a worldly man and a marginal Christian at best, was greatly personally impacted by the relationship that he had had with the late Father Herman. Yanovsky sent to the Abbot two letters that Herman had written to him: his intention was to make the life that this holy man had led known to the whole world.

In 1867 the Abbot received a response from the Archbishop of Kamchatka and the Aleutians. The Archbishop attested to his deliverance from drowning through the intercessory prayers of Father Herman; this confirmed the report of Gerasim's friend in 1864. In addition, the Abbot also got an answer from the Vicar of the Kamchatka diocese. Bishop Peter sent him information on Herman collected by a Kodiak priest, Constantine Larionev. It is significant that all of this information was collected exactly 30 years after St. Herman's death, exactly as he had predicted.

On March 11, 1969 the Great Council of Bishops of the Orthodox Church in America declared its intention to canonize Herman. On August 9, 1970 St. Herman was canonized in a ceremony in Kodiak, Alaska.

Excellent resources on the life of Saint Herman include Frank Alfred Golder, *Father Herman, Alaska's Saint; A Preliminary Account of the Life and Miracles of Blessed Father Herman*;[16] Father Seraphim Rose and Abbot Herman Podmoshensky, compilers and translators, *Northern Thebaid: Monastic Saints of the Russian North*.[17] Bishop Alexander Mileant, ed., "Saint Herman of Alaska," is an online article that provides a compilation of excerpts taken from primary sources-it includes Herman, *Letter to Baranoff, 1809*; Herman, *Letter of June 20, 1820*; Yanovsky, *Letter of November 22, 1865*; Yanovsky, *Life of Monk Herman in Valaam*;

Archpriest Prokopy Povarnitsyn's stories of miraculous healings that he gathered from the Aleuts in the 1930s and 1940s during his stay in Alaska.[18] Another online article is "Glorification of the Venerable Herman of Alaska, Wonderworker of all America."[19]

THE TRANSFIGURATION OF
SAINT SERAPHIM OF SAROV

Born Prohor Moshnin in Kursk, Russia (1759-1833), Saint Seraphim of Sarov was a deeply devout and pious Orthodox Christian from his youth. God, who sees into the future and knows all people from their mothers' wombs, loved and blessed Prohor with miraculous healings and visions of the Lord and His saints from his childhood.

When Prohor was young, the Virgin Mary miraculously healed him several times from his illnesses. At the age of 10, he became very sick, but he saw Mary in a dream and she promised him that she would restore his health. Soon afterwards, a religious procession, one in which a miracle-working icon of Mary was held up and revered, was traveling through his city. Inclement weather caused the leaders of the procession to take an alternate route and they ended up walking past Prohor's home. His mother brought him over to the icon and he was miraculously healed.

Prohor was to be divinely healed again in his teen years. At 18 he entered a monastery in Sarov as a novice. He became sick once more and Mary healed him again. Bishop Alexander Mileant, in his article, "St. Seraphim of Sarov: Life and Teachings," describes the event thus:

> St. Seraphim was once again healed by the Most Holy Virgin Mary, Who appeared to him accompanied by several saints. Pointing to the venerable Seraphim, The Holy Virgin said to the apostle John the Theologian: "He

is of our lineage." Then, by touching his side with Her staff, She healed him.[20]

Mary's declaration, "He is of our lineage," is highly significant. She was speaking to John the apostle, author of the Gospel of John, to whom the Lord entrusted her when He was on the Cross. When Jesus had completed His mission on earth, He wanted John to care for His mother because He did not have any brothers or sisters: "When Jesus therefore saw his mother, and the disciple standing by, whom he loved, he saith unto his mother, Woman, behold thy son! Then saith he to the disciple, Behold thy mother! And from that hour that disciple took her unto his own home" (John 19:26-27). Hence, John became Mary's adopted son from that moment on. That was in 33 AD.

Now, in the latter half of the eighteenth century, Mary also makes a declaration of adoption: she tells John that Prohor is of "our lineage." From that moment forward, Prohor is adopted into the spiritual family of Mary and John. It is not a biological family, but one of a spiritual, eternal communion. Henceforth, Mary would be his spiritual mother and John, his spiritual brother. Mary's declaration is an affirmation of Prohor's status as a member of God's eternal family. Jesus was to become the firstborn among many brethren; these brethren are those who are conformed to the image of the Son (Rom 8:29).

Prohor was tonsured as a monk in 1786 at the age of 27. Upon becoming a monk, he was given the name Seraphim, which in Hebrew means "fiery" or "burning." Indeed, this aptly fit his passion for the things belonging to God and his desire to give up everything to follow Christ. God, who could see into Seraphim's heart, knew that he was earnestly seeking Him and He also found purity there. Christ advised, "Blessed are the pure in heart: for they shall see God" (Mat 5:8). Indeed, Seraphim's life is an iconic representation of this truth: Bishop Mileant recounts the fact that Seraphim saw Christ and His angels in church:

> He spent all of his time, save for the very shortest of rests, in church. Through such prayer and the labors of religious services, Seraphim became worthy to see angels, both serving and singing in church. During the liturgy on Holy Thursday, he saw the Lord Jesus Christ Himself, in the form of the Son of man, proceeding into the Church with the Heavenly host and blessing those praying. The saint could not speak for a long time after being struck by this vision.[21]

The fact that the Holy Spirit was made manifest in Seraphim is seen in the fact that the wildest animals in the forest, bears, foxes, and wolves, all became as tame as kittens when they approached him. The elder nun of the Diveevo monastery, Mother Plescheeva, witnessed the total transformation of the nature of a wild bear who meekly ate out of Seraphim's hand. It is significant that when this occurred, Seraphim's face was illumined and glowing, much like that of the Lord during His Transfiguration on Mount Tabor:

> The *staritsa* (i.e., eldress) of the Diveevo monastery, Matrona Plescheeva, witnessed how St. Seraphim fed a bear that had come to him out of his hand: "The face of the great starets was particularly miraculous. It was joyous and bright, as that of an angel," she described.[22]

Here we see that the Holy Spirit was made manifest in Seraphim: the evidence was that wild animals were rendered tame and Seraphim's face shone like the sun.

This transformation, both in the nature of animals and in the physical appearance of humans, has antecedents in the Bible. In the OT evidence of the presence of the Holy Spirit and His transformative power is as follows: the wolf will dwell with the lamb; the leopard will lie down with the kid; the calf and the young lion and the fatling together; a little child shall lead all of these formerly wild animals that include the leopard and the young lion (Is 11:6). Furthermore, the cow and the bear will feed together; their young ones will lie down together; the formerly carnivorous lion will eat straw like the ox (Is 11:7). In addition, little children will play on the hole of the asp and will put their hands in the adder's den (Is 11:8). This is all evidence of the presence of the Holy Spirit on earth. St. Seraphim, filled with the Holy Spirit, performed similar miracles when he fed a bear out of the palm of his hand.

Moreover, he, himself, was physically transformed and his face was joyous and bright as that of an angel. This sounds like the transfiguration of St. Stephen, whose face also became luminous. Stephen was brought before a counsel and falsely accused of blasphemy: "And all that sat in the council, looking stedfastly on him, saw his face as it had been the face of an angel" (Acts 6:15). This implies that his face shone with light.

Mention should also be made of the fact that when Moses came down from Mount Sinai carrying the two tablets in his hands, his face was radiant because he had been speaking to God (Ex 34:29). Then Moses spoke to the people, and having done so, he proceeded to cover his face with a veil. He removed the veil when he entered the Lord's presence, but then put it on again when he spoke to the people (Ex 34:30-35).

Paul reflects on the significance of Moses' actions to cover his face with a veil when standing before the people (2 Cor 3:7-18). Paul points out that the radiance of Moses' face was fading and that it was not permanent. Similarly, the Old Covenant that God made was to be temporary and merely a foreshadowing of the New

Covenant that was promised in Jer 31:31-32. Paul advises that the reason that Moses covered his face with a veil was so that the people would not see that his radiance was gradually fading (2 Cor 3:13). His radiance was temporary, as the Old Covenant was to be temporary. Paul exhorts his listeners to recognize that they, New Covenant believers, have something much better than Moses' temporary radiance: they are indwelt by the Holy Spirit. All of the promises of the OT have come to fruition in Christ Jesus: what was glorious in Moses' time has been far surpassed by the glory of the present age (2 Cor 3:10-11). When people choose to follow Christ, the veil is taken away (2 Cor 3:16). The Holy Spirit indwells the Christian and brings freedom from sin (2 Cor 3:17). We, Christians, under the New Covenant, stand with unveiled faces and reflect God's glory: "But we all, with open face beholding as in a glass the glory of the Lord, are changed into the same image from glory to glory, even as by the Spirit of the Lord" (2 Cor 3:18).

Hence, the illumination of Seraphim's face as he tamed wild bears was evidence that he was filled with the Holy Spirit. This transfiguration would happen again in his life.

In 1804, at the age of 45, Seraphim was brutally attacked by thieves who beat him with the handle of his own axe. Because of the injuries that he received from his assailants, he was left permanently crippled: he spent the remainder of his life hunched over and he could walk only with the help of a staff. When his attackers were finally apprehended and brought before a judge, this holy man argued clemency on their behalf.

Statues of St. Seraphim often portray him kneeling on a stone with his hands raised towards Heaven. This is because he prayed continuously for 1,000 days and nights. He led a very austere and disciplined life of continual prayer and fasting. In his biography of the Saint, Bishop Mileant advises, "...he spent his days on a rock near his little hermitage, and nights in the thick of the forest. He prayed with his arms raised to heaven, almost without respite. This feat of his continued for a thousand days."[23] Today there is a statue of St. Seraphim at the Korennaya monastery in Kursk. The Saint is depicted in his monastic habit, wearing the copper cross that his mother had given him when he left home to enter the monastery, kneeling on a stone, praying with his hands raised towards Heaven, as he had done for 1,000 days and nights.

Having prayed like this, for 1,000 days and nights, outdoors, and despite inclement weather, St. Seraphim had a vision of Mary. In this vision, she entreated him to agree to become a spiritual elder (*starets*), or one who advises others in their Christian walk. As an elder, St. Seraphim received many special gifts from God. One of them was clairvoyance: he was not only able to advise people as to the best course of action to take, he even knew what questions they would ask even before they opened their mouth.

Then, towards the end of his life, in November of 1831, the most fascinating, astounding miracle of all happened: the Saint's countenance was miraculously transfigured into dazzling light, brighter than the sun, before his disciple, Nicholas Motovilov. It was a dreary, gloomy fall day when Motovilov had come to visit Seraphim near his hermitage. He had a philosophical question on his mind, one that he had been wondering about for most of his life. Even before Motovilov had the chance to ask the question, Seraphim already knew what it was. The question was this: what is the meaning of the Christian life and why do Christians live on earth? St. Seraphim was ready with the answer: the true aim of the Christian life is to acquire the Holy Spirit of God.

At this point, Motovilov asked his mentor how he could see the grace of the Holy Spirit. He asked how he could really know, once and for all, whether the Holy Spirit was with him or not.

After he had posed this question several times St. Seraphim was miraculously transfigured as the Lord had been on Mount Tabor. Seraphim whole body shone with dazzling light like the sun and Motovilov understood the transformative power of the Holy Spirit. He also knew that the Holy Spirit was with him because he and his teacher were bathed in His light and he felt a peace and joy in his heart that he had never experienced before.

After this miracle occurred, Motovilov recorded it in the form of notes. His notes were later transcribed and published by Sergius Nilus, along with an introduction. Georgy Petrovich Fedotov's *A Treasury of Russian Spirituality*, a true cornucopia of translations of original texts, contains *A Conversation of St. Seraphim of Sarov with Nicholas Motovilov concerning the Aim of the Christian Life*. The highlights of Motovilov's account are as follows:

"The Lord has revealed to me," began the great elder, "that in your childhood you longed to know the aim of our Christian life and continually asked questions about it of many and great ecclesiastical dignitaries."

Let me here interpose that from the age of twelve this thought had ceaselessly vexed me, and I had, in fact, approached many clergy about it; but their answers had not satisfied me. This was not known to the elder.

"But no one," continued Father Seraphim, "has given you a precise answer...The true aim of our Christian life, is to acquire the Holy Spirit of God..."

"But, father...How am I going to know whether He is with me or not?"...

"How can I myself recognize His true manifestation?"...

Then Father Seraphim took me very firmly by the shoulders and said:

"We are both together, son, in the Spirit of God! Why lookest thou not on me?"

"I replied: "I cannot look, father, because lightning flashes from your eyes. Your face is brighter than the sun and my eyes ache in pain!"

Father Seraphim said: "Fear not, my son; you too have become as bright as I. You too are now in the fullness of God's Spirit; otherwise you would not be able to look on me as I am."...

After these words I looked in his face and there came over me an even greater reverential awe. Imagine in the centre of the sun, in the dazzling brilliance of his midday rays, the face of the man who talks with you. You see the movement of his lips and the changing expression of his eyes, you hear his voice, you feel someone grasp your shoulders; yet you do not see the hands, you do not even see yourself or his figure, but only a blinding light spreading several yards around and throwing a sparkling radiance across the snow blanket on the glade and into the snowflakes which besprinkled the great elder and me....

"This...is that peace of which the Lord said to His disciples: My peace I give unto you; not as the world giveth, give I unto you [John 14:27]...the peace which... passeth all understanding [Phil 4:7]....

"When the Spirit of God descends to man and overshadows him with the fulness of His outpouring, then the human soul overflows with unspeakable joy, because the Spirit of God turns to joy all that He may touch…"[24]

There are a few salient points here that deserve mention. First, God has granted Seraphim the gift of clairvoyance so that he may glorify Him by assisting others. Seraphim is able to discern what is uppermost in the inquirer's mind even before he speaks. This is clearly evidence of the presence of the Holy Spirit. It also provides proof that a spiritual realm does, indeed, exist, and that people who have acquired this gift of clairvoyance from God, can and do communicate with one another within this spiritual realm, without the need for words.

Secondly, there is a deeply personal relationship between the spiritual elder (*starets*) and his disciple. The elder focuses his attention to meeting the spiritual needs of the particular person to whom he is talking. The relationship, then, between the elder and the disciple is intensely personal. Bishop Kallistos Ware, in *The Orthodox Way*, describes the unique bond between the teacher and student thus:

> Always the relationship is personal. The *starets* does not apply abstract rules learnt from a book-as in the "casuistry" of Counter-Reformation Catholicism-but he sees on each occasion this particular man or woman who is before him; and, illumined by the Spirit, he seeks to transmit the unique will of God specifically for this one person. Because the true *starets* understands and respects the distinctive character of each one, he does not suppress their inward freedom but reinforces it. He does not aim at eliciting a mechanical obedience, but leads his children to the point of spiritual maturity where they can decide for themselves. To each one he shows his or her true face, which before was largely hidden from that person; and

his word is creative and life-giving, enabling the other to accomplish tasks which previously seemed impossible.[25]

Moreover, Seraphim requested that one day, after he died, that people would come to his grave and kneel down and tell him what is on their minds. Christians are immortal and so, he promises that he will continue to listen to them. Seraphim wanted the following epitaph to appear on his tombstone:

> When I am dead, come to me at my grave, and the more often the better. Whatever is on your soul, whatever may have happened to you, come to me as when I was alive, and kneeling on the ground, cast all your bitterness upon my grave. Tell me everything and I shall listen to you, and all the bitterness will fly away from you. And as you spoke to me when I was alive, do so now. For I am living, and I shall be for ever.[26]

Thirdly, and most significantly, God the Father provided Motovilov with physical evidence of His existence: He sent His Holy Spirit to manifest Himself both within his physical body and without. Both the elder and his disciple are bathed in blinding, brilliant light emanating from the spiritual realm, much like the face of Moses when he came down from Mount Sinai holding the two tablets in his hands (Ex 34:29-35; 2 Cor 3:7-18); the Transfiguration of Christ, Moses, and Elijah on Mount Tabor on the Feast of Tabernacles (Mat 17:1-9; Mark 9:2-9; Luke 9:28-36); the transfiguration of Stephen (Acts 6:15); the Lord's appearance to Saul on the road to Damascus (Acts 9:1-19; 22:3-16; 26:9-18; 1 Cor 9:1).

The life of St. Seraphim provides a living, breathing, concrete illustration of the Lord's words, "Blessed are the pure in heart: for they shall see God"; of the fact that the Lord's Transfiguration on Mount Tabor was a preview of what awaits every Christian who achieves theosis; of the powerful change that occurs in the mind, heart, soul, and even the physical body of the person who gives up everything to follow Christ diligently pursues His Kingdom.

To date, there exists a wealth of resources on St. Seraphim. We recommend A.M. Allchin, *Wholeness and Transfiguration: Illustrated in the Lives of St. Francis of Assisi and St. Seraphim of Sarov;*[27] Julia de Beausobre, *Flame in the Snow: A Life of St. Seraphim of Sarov;*[28] Harry M. Boosalis, *Joy of the Holy: St. Seraphim of Sarov and Orthodox Spiritual Life;*[29] Paul Evdokimov, *St. Seraphim of Sarov: An Icon of Orthodox Spirituality;*[30] Irina Gorainoff, *Séraphim de Sarov;*[31] Ivan Kologrivof, *Essai sur la sainteté en Russie;*[32] Helen Kontzevitch, *Saint Seraphim: Wonderworker of Sarov;*[33] Louis-Albert Lassus, *Staretz Séraphim de Sarov: joie et lumière;*[34] Bishop Alexander Mileant's Internet articles, "Saint Seraphim of Sarov: On Acquisition of the Holy Spirit"[35] and "St. Seraphim of Sarov: Life and Teachings";[36] Nicholas Motovilov, *A Conversation of St. Seraphim of Sarov with Nicholas Motovilov concerning the Aim of the Christian Life;*[37] Vsévolod Rochcau, *Saint Séraphim, Sarov et Divéyevo: études et documents, suivis d'une étude sur un fragment inédit des Récits d'un pèlerin russe;*[38] Valentine Zander, *St. Seraphim of Sarov.*[39]

THE MIRACULOUS ICON OF MARY ON THE GREEK ISLAND OF TINOS

Just as the Greek War of Independence against Turkish rule was underway in 1821, the Virgin Mary appeared to a nun, Pelagia, in her sleep, on the island of Tinos. Mary told Pelagia that a holy icon was buried in the ground and she gave her instructions as to where to find it. Pelagia related the dream to her abbess and soon excavation began. In 1823 a Byzantine church dedicated to St. John the Baptist was unearthed at the site and along with it, the icon that Mary had described in Pelagia's dream. The icon began performing miracles and soon many pilgrims traveled to the newly established shrine at that location seeking miraculous cures of healing. By 1830 a new church, comprised of two levels, was completed. When the bishop consecrated the cornerstone, a dry well that was on the site miraculously filled with water and healed the sick. In addition, the discovery of the icon did bring the Greeks the much hoped for liberation from Turkish rule: the Greek War of Independence, lasting from March 1821 until July 1832, resulted in the establishment of an independence kingdom of Greece. In 1970 Pelagia was canonized. St. Pelagia's feast day is celebrated on July 23 in the Kechrovouni Convent and the cell in which she lived is open to visitors today. Her cell is a simple room with a tiny wooden bed and a chest.[40]

John Freely, in his travel book, *The Cyclades: Discovering the Greek Islands of the Aegean*, briefly summarizes the discovery of the miraculous icon of Tinos thus:

> During the first year of the Greek War of Independence a Tinian nun named Pelagia had a dream in which the Virgin revealed to her the location of a miraculous icon. The next morning Pelagia told the prioress of the convent about her dream, and soon afterwards the locals unearthed the icon at the spot where the Virgin had indicated that it was buried, on a farm just above the port town of Agios Nikolaus, the present Chora. The discovery of the icon caused great excitement among the Tiniotes, particularly after several miraculous cures were attributed to it. An extensive church complex was then erected on the site to house the icon of the Evangelistria, known as Panaghia Megalochari, the Virgin of Great Joy, and pilgrims from all over the Greek world began congregating there on the Virgin's two annual feast days.[41]

MIRACLES OF ST. ARSENIOS OF PAROS
DURING HIS LIFE AND AFTER HIS REPOSE

St. Arsenios of Paros (1800-1877) was a monk, Orthodox priest, teacher, and miracle worker who lived on the island of Paros in the Aegean. As a priest, St. Arsenios was overseer of the nuns at the Holy Convent of the Transfiguration of Christ on Paros. He performed many miracles of healing for people who were incurably ill and dying, both during his life and after his death. In addition, his spirit was seen walking about the convent after his death. The Synod of the Ecumenical Patriarchate at Constantinople declared Arsenios to be a saint in 1967, ninety years after his death.

Dr. Constantine Cavarnos has written a biography of the saint for the English-speaking world, entitled, *St. Arsenios of Paros: Remarkable Confessor, Spiritual Guide, Educator, Ascetic, Miracle-worker, and Healer; An Account of His Life, Character, Message and Miracles.*[42] Cavarnos derives much of his biographical material from an account of the saint written in Greek by Archimandrite Philotheos Zervakos, entitled, *The Life, Conduct, and Miracles of Our Father Arsenios the New, Who Led a Life of Spiritual Endeavor on the Island of Paros [Bios, Politeia, kai Thaumata tou Patros Hemon Arseniou tou Neou tou en te Neso Paro Askesantos].*[43] Zervakos was the Abbot of the Monastery of Longovarda in Paros; he died in 1980. Zervakos substantiates the historicity of the miracles that the holy saint performed by including dates, names, and places surrounding the events (ie: the names of parents and spouses of the sick, and the names of surgeons and the hospitals and cities in which they practiced medicine). These details establish that the factual basis of each miracle is certain.

St. Arsenios was a teacher during the years 1829-1840. He became a monk, joining the Monastery of Saint George, was ordained a deacon at 29, and became a presbyter at 47. It was around the time that he was ordained a priest that he received the gift of tears, that is, the continual shedding of tears (*katanyxis*). Orthodoxy teaches that this is an accompaniment of prayer and that it leads to the purification of thought and heart. Cavarnos describes the gift thus, deriving information from the *Philokalia*:

> And Theophanes the Monk, author of a remarkable "Ladder of Divine Gifts," which is included in the *Philokalia*, views tears as an accompaniment of pure prayer, i.e., of undistracted mental prayer, and having in their turn as accompaniments peace of thoughts and purification of the mind. Pure prayer, he says, leads to warmth of the heart, warmth of the heart, to holy inward action; holy inward action, to heartfelt tears; heartfelt tears, to peace of thoughts of every sort, and peace of thoughts, to purification of the mind.[44]

Let us take a look at what Theophanis the Monk, in "The Ladder of Divine Graces," says about the divine gift of the continual shedding of tears. He begins by describing man's ascent towards holiness:

> The first step is that of purest prayer.
> From this there comes a warmth of heart,
> And then a strange, a holy energy,
> Then tears wrung from the heart, God-given.
> Then peace from thoughts of every kind.
> From this arises purging of the intellect,
> And next the vision of heavenly mysteries.
> Unheard-of-light is born from this ineffably,
> And thence, beyond all telling, the heart's illumination.
> Last comes a step that has no limit
> Though compassed into a single line-
> Perfection that is endless.[45]

Having demonstrated that the divine gift of tears is a step on a ladder leading towards perfection, Cavarnos indicates that God, having bestowed this particular gift upon Arsenios, went on to grant him many more. Cavarnos enumerates the multiple blessings that the saint received: he intuitively knew the thoughts of others; he received the gift of foreknowledge; he was able to perform miracles, including miracles of healing. Cavarnos' source, Archimandrite Zervakos, relates instances of foreknowledge (such as that of an impending fire), mind-reading (while administering the sacrament of confession to a penitent who did not confess everything), and miraculous cures (including that of tuberculosis) performed by the saint both during his lifetime and after his death.[46]

In addition to these divine gifts, Arsenios also had an encounter with a departed saint who disapproved of his behavior and advised him to repent. It was on this occasion that he met St. George the Martyr on the road en route to the Monastery of St. George. Arsenios had been deeply disturbed by the nuns at the Holy Convent of the Transfiguration of Christ because of their uncharitable behavior towards one another. Because they had been quarreling and bickering among themselves, he resolved to pack his bags and leave. Having left the convent, he was en route to the Monastery of St. George when St. George appeared to him in the form of a young man. St. George commanded Arsenios not to abandon the nuns because of their faults. He told him, "And how come you did not reflect that our Lord endures the misbehavior of millions of men, even of those who do not believe in Him, but insult Him, blaspheme Him, despise Him, and endured even those who crucified Him, and while on the Cross He prayed for His crucifiers, saying: 'Father, forgive them, for they know not what they do?' Why is that you cannot endure the wrong acts of forty monastics, who…now have repented?"[47]

Arsenios scoffed at the admonishment and refused to go back. At that point St. George revealed two things to him: first, a resplendent, beautiful light on his right hand side, and then a thick darkness replete with a piercing, foul smell on his left. George advised Arsenios that if he forgave the nuns their sins and returned to the convent, the beautiful light would follow him the rest of his life and remain with him, even as he entered the Kingdom of Heaven. However, if he refused to forgive these unfortunate sinners whom God had entrusted to his care, then the palpable, foul-smelling darkness would remain with him and follow him into hell.

The young man's face flashed like lightening and then he disappeared. At this point Arsenios recognized him as St. George the Martyr and he repented of the sin of unforgiveness. He forgave the nuns in his heart and returned to the convent. It is important to remember that Arsenios was a priest who was overseeing the nuns. We can see that his inability to forgive the shortcomings of others as an ordained priest and representative of Christ on earth was a serious sin in the eyes of God. In a parable Christ advised, "And that servant, which knew his lord's will, and prepared not himself, neither did according to his will, shall be beaten with many stripes…For unto whomsoever much is given, of him shall be much required: and to whom men have committed much, of him they will ask the more" (Luke 12:47-48).

When Arsenios returned to the convent, he saw that the nuns had repented of their uncharitable behavior and were relieved that he had returned to forgive them, lest they die unforgiven. In addition to the miraculous appearance of St. George en route to the monastery, Cavernos cites 14 miracles that Arsenios performed and that are recorded by Archimandrite Zervakos: 6 miracles while he lived and 8 after the died. Cavarnos explains, "The Lord says: 'I shall glorify those who glorify me.' Because

St. Arsenios glorified God while he lived on earth through the observance of His commandments, the achievements of the virtues and the performance of good works, God glorified him and gave him the power and grace to perform many miracles both before and after his death."⁴⁸ Briefly, the miracles that Arsenios performed before his death can be summarized thus:

1. There was a drought on the island of Paros. As the village watched, Arsenios knelt and prayed. Then he said, "Run quickly, lest you be still on the way when it starts to rain." The sky darkened and there was a tremendous downpour.⁴⁹

2. A similar miracle occurred again when there was a drought at the Holy Convent of the Transfiguration of Christ. The inhabitants of Paroikia asked him to pay, he did, and the drought immediately ended.⁵⁰

3. A sister of one of the nuns became very ill. It was feared that she might have the plague, which had recently appeared on the island. When Arsenios prayed over her, she immediately recovered.⁵¹

4. This miracle occurred on Mt. Athos. When Arsenios was a little boy, he and the Elder Daniel set out to visit the brothers at the skete of Iviron. En route, the young Arsenios advised the Elder Daniel that they should take a different road and foretold that if they were to remain on their chosen path, their lives would be in grave danger. Daniel ignored Arsenios' warning and continued on the same road. It was not long before they found themselves confronted by a fire which quickly grew and surrounded them. Arsenios was able to escape unhurt; however, Daniel suffered an injury to his leg and the resulting scar remained with him the rest of his life.⁵²

5. When Arsenios was a priest at the Holy Convent of the Transfiguration of Christ, a certain man went there to receive the sacrament of confession. However, the

penitent confessed all of his sins, except one, to the priest. Arsenios asked him, "Have you confessed all of your sins?" The man replied that he had done so. Arsenios countered, "But you have not confessed the stealing of the lemons." The man was struck by the fact that his confessor knew about this one and knelt down, in tears, asking for forgiveness. Upon leaving, he informed all the others who were waiting to see the priest that Arsenios knew everyone's sins and that he would reveal them. Word got around and thereafter, penitents took care to be thorough in their confessions.[53]

6. Another account of a miraculous healing performed by St. Arsenios while he was still alive is related by his disciple, Hieromonk Nikolaos Georgiadis. The miracle involves a young relative of Arsenios who was dying of tuberculosis. Cavarnos describes the young man thus: "…and looked like a shadow, an unburned corpse." The young man and his father traveled from Epirus to Paros to see Arsenios. When Arsenios met the young man, he noticed that he was wearing a cloak called a *kappa*. Arsenios admired the cloak and asked to borrow it for a moment: "You are wearing a very beautiful *kappa*! Won't you give it to me to put on?" Arsenios put it on and wore it only for two minutes. Then he returned the cloak to the young man. As soon as the youth put it on, he was instantly healed of his disease: his complexion changed and became ruddy; he regained his strength; he returned home in full health.[54]

Cavarnos goes on to enumerate several miracles that the saint performed after his death:

1. A certain woman had a child who had been born blind. She took her son to the tomb of St. Arsenios and prayed that the saint would intercede and restore her child's

sight. After they left the tomb, the child picked up a needle from the ground and held it up to his mother and asked, "What is this, mother?" It was then that she noticed that her child's closed eyes had been opened and that his sight had been restored.[55]

2. Another woman, from the city of Angeria on the island of Paros, had a child who was paralyzed. She took her child to St. Arsenios' tomb and prayed there. Immediately at the end of the prayer, the child arose and began to walk for the first time.[56]

3. One night a gang of thieves invaded the island of Paros and stood defiantly outside the Holy Convent of the Transfiguration of Christ. They shouted to the nuns inside that they wanted to enter and demanded that the nuns prepare to turn over to them all of their valuables, as well as the young nuns in the convent. Frightened, the nuns and their abbess prayed to St. Arsenios for protection. Then the thieves shouted that if they did not open the door, they would set a fire and burn down the convent. The nuns opened the door and the brigands entered. However, after taking a few steps, the marauders became paralyzed in their tracks and were unable to move. It was this miracle that instilled the fear of God in them and caused them to repent of their sins. They begged for mercy from the saint who protected the convent and promised to give the nuns all of the valuables that they had as a gift in return for their forgiveness and release. The abbess held up a cross and crossed them and they were released from their paralysis. The leader and his gang bowed low to the nuns, kissed the hand of the abbess, and gave them all of their possessions. The life of the leader of the gang was forever changed by the miracle: not only did he repent of his sins, he left the group and became tonsured as a monk. This account is particularly striking because it involves both a miracle of protection from harm, as well

as a change of heart in a criminal who turns to Christ and surrenders his life to Him.[57]

4. The young nephew of one of the nuns at the convent, Theophano Vazaiou, came to visit his aunt. That night, while sitting outside the chapel, the boy saw an elderly man who resembled perfectly the picture of St. Arsenios on his icon. This elderly figure came out of the door of the chapel, walked around the convent once with his walking stick, and then went back inside and closed the door. The following morning the child related to the nuns what he had seen. Because there were no elders that had been visiting at the church at the time, the nuns immediately understood that St. Arsenios was ever present and watching over their convent.[58]

5. This miracle was written in the first person singular: it is understood that the narrator, "I," is Archimandrite Philotheos Zervakos, from whose text Cavarnos quotes. Therefore, this striking testimonial provides an eyewitness account in the first person of a miracle of healing that St. Arsenios performed after his death. In July-August 1925 Archimandrite Zervakos was stricken by malaria and the doctors at the chief hospital in Athens did not believe that he would survive. Arsenios' disciple, Hieromonk Nikolaos Georgiadis, went to the tomb of St. Arsenios and prayed for him. He prayed for an hour and then felt that the saint was telling him in his heart, "Go your way now, the sick man has been cured." Concurrently, Zervakos, on his deathbed in the hospital, felt his strength return and his health was restored.[59]

6. On August 10, 1952, the newspaper, *The Voice of Paros*, published an article that was a testimonial to the healing intercessory power of St. Arsenios. The author of the article, a teacher by the name of Nikolaos Kritikos, related how his daughter had been dying of paratyphoid in August 1946. Paratyphoid is caused by salmonellae

bacteria that resemble the typhoid bacterium and cause a disease milder than typhoid fever. The girl's physician, Doctor Kastanos, gave up on her and advised him to prepare his wife for the imminent demise of their daughter. However, the nuns of the Holy Convent of the Transfiguration of Christ conducted a prayer of entreaty [*paraklesis*] and asked St. Arsenios for help. On Sunday the girl was anointed with holy oil from the lamp of St. Arsenios at the convent's church. It was then that her breathing became normalized, her heartbeat regular, and that she was miraculously cured of the paratyphoid.[60]

7. The historicity of this miracle is also made certain by names, places, and dates. In 1960 a woman by the name of Helen Bargiamis, 56 years old, was dying of breast cancer in Piraeus. Her condition worsened and the doctors at the clinic in Piraeus prognosed that her death was imminent. Because she liked the monastic life, she wanted to be tonsured as a nun so that she might die as one. During the ceremony, St. Arsenios appeared at her bedside, dressed in his humble vestments. He walked past the priest and then stood beneath his holy icon. Then he suddenly vanished. After that she went to the hospital where her health was miraculously restored and she walked out of the hospital fully recovered.[61]

8. On January 30, 1976, the day prior to the Feast Day of St. Arsenios, Metropolitan Amurosios was forced to remain in bed because of very painful kidney stones. He prayed to St Arsenios for help and when he did, the kidney stone what was causing him excruciating pain suddenly passed. The Metropolitan was cured and was able to preside in church on the feast day of the saint.[62]

Endnotes

1   Constantine Cavarnos, *St. Macarios of Corinth: Archbishop of Corinth, Guardian of Sacred Tradition, Reviver of Orthodox Mysticism, Compiler of the Philokalia, Spiritual Striver, Enlightener and Guide, and Trainer of Martyrs: An Account of His Life, Character and Message, Together with Selections from Three of His Publications* (Belmont, MA: Institute for Byzantine and Modern Greek Studies, 1972).

2   Athanasios Parios, *Akoluthia of Our Father Saint Macarios Notaras, Archbishop of Corinth* (Chios, 1863).

3   Constantine Cavarnos, *St. Macarios of Corinth: Archbishop of Corinth, Guardian of Sacred Tradition, Reviver of Orthodox Mysticism, Compiler of the Philokalia, Spiritual Striver, Enlightener and Guide, and Trainer of Martyrs: An Account of His Life, Character and Message, Together with Selections from Three of His Publications* (Belmont, MA: Institute for Byzantine and Modern Greek Studies, 1972), 67-69.

4   Ibid., 69-70.

5   Ibid., 71.

6   Ibid., 72-73.

7   Constantine Cavarnos, *St. Nikephoros of Chios: Outstanding Writer of Liturgical Poetry and Lives of Saints, Educator, Spiritual Striver, and Trainer of Martyrs: An Account of His Life, Character and Message, Together with a Comprehensive List of His Publications, Selections from Them, and Brief Biographies of Eleven Neomartyrs and Other Orthodox Saints Who are Treated in His Works* (Belmont: Institute for Byzantine and Modern Greek Studies, 1976).

8   Emily Sarou, *The Life of St. Nikephoros*, in *New Chian Leimonation [Neon Chiakon Leimonarion]* (Athens, 1968), 199-203.

9   Constantine Cavarnos, *St. Nikephoros of Chios: Outstanding Writer of Liturgical Poetry and Lives of Saints, Educator, Spiritual Striver, and Trainer of Martyrs: An Account of His Life, Character and Message, Together with a Comprehensive List of His Publications, Selections from Them, and Brief Biographies of Eleven Neomartyrs and Other Orthodox Saints Who are Treated in His Works* (Belmont: Institute for Byzantine and Modern Greek Studies, 1976), 59.

10 Ibid.

11 Ibid.

12 Ibid., 59-60.

13 Ibid., 60-61.

14 Ibid., 61.

15 Ibid., 62-63.

16 Frank Alfred Golder, *Father Herman, Alaska's Saint; A Preliminary Account of the Life and Miracles of Blessed Father Herman* (Willits: Eastern Orthodox Books, 1972).

17 Father Seraphim Rose and Abbot Herman Podmoshensky, compilers and translators, *Northern Thebaid: Monastic Saints of the Russian North* (Platina: Saint Herman Press, 1995).

18 Bishop Alexander Mileant, ed., "Saint Herman of Alaska," http://www.fatheralexander.org/ booklets/english/herman.htm (March 18, 2008).

19 "Glorification of the Venerable Herman of Alaska, Wonderworker of All America." http://www.ocafs.oca.org/FeastSaintsLife.asp?FSID =102241 (March 18, 2008).

20 Bishop Alexander Mileant, "St. Seraphim of Sarov: Life and Teachings," translated by Nicholas and Natalia Semyanko, http://www.fatheralexander.org/booklets/english/seraphim_e. htm (February 29, 2008).

21 Ibid.

22 Ibid.

23 Ibid.

24 Nicholas Motovilov, *A Conversation of St. Seraphim of Sarov with Nicholas Motovilov concerning the Aim of the Christian Life*, in "Georgy Petrovich Fedotov, ed., *A Treasury of Russian Spirituality* (Mineola: Dover Publications, Inc., 2003), 266-75. This book is available online at http://www.holytrinitymission.org/books/english/ russian_spirituality_fedotov. htm (March 4, 2008).

25 Bishop Kallistos Ware, *The Orthodox Way*, revised edition (Crestwood: St. Vladimir's Seminary Press, 1995), 96-97.

26 Ibid., 98 [Irina Gorainoff, *Séraphim de Sarov* (Bégrolles-en-Mauges: Abbaye de Bellefontaine, 1973), 133-34].

27 A.M. Allchin, *Wholeness and Transfiguration: Illustrated in the Lives of St. Francis of Assisi and St. Seraphim of Sarov* (Fairacres, Oxford: SLG Press, The Convent of the Incarnation, 1974).

28 Julia de Beausobre, *Flame in the Snow: A Life of St. Seraphim of Sarov* (Springfield: Templegate Publishers, 1996).

29 Harry M. Boosalis, *Joy of the Holy: St. Seraphim of Sarov and Orthodox Spiritual Life* (South Canaan: St. Tikhon'Seminary Press, 1993).

30 Paul Evdokimov, *St. Seraphim of Sarov: An Icon of Orthodox Spirituality* (Minneapolis: Light and Life Publishing Company, Inc., 1988).

31 Irina Gorainoff, *Séraphim de Sarov* (Bégrolles-en-Mauges: Abbaye de Bellefontaine, 1973).

32 Ivan Kologrivof, *Essai sur la sainteté en Russie* (Bruges: Beyaert, 1953).

33 Helen Kontzevitch, *Saint Seraphim: Wonderworker of Sarov*, translated by St. Xenia Skete (Wildwood: Saint Xenia Skete, 2004).

34 Louis-Albert Lassus, *Staretz Séraphim de Sarov: joie et lumière* (Paris: O.E.I.L., 1984).

35 Bishop Alexander Mileant, "Saint Seraphim of Sarov: On Acquisition of the Holy Spirit," http://www.fatheralexander.org/booklets/english/sermon_st_seraphim.htm (February 29, 2008).

36 Bishop Alexander Mileant, "St. Seraphim of Sarov: Life and Teachings," translated by Nicholas and Natalia Semyanko, http://www.fatheralexander.org/booklets/english/seraphim_e. htm (February 29, 2008).

37 Nicholas Motovilov, *A Conversation of St. Seraphim of Sarov with Nicholas Motovilov concerning the Aim of the Christian Life*, in Georgy Petrovich Fedotov, ed., *A Treasury of Russian Spirituality* (Mineola: Dover Publications, Inc., 2003), 266-79. This book is available online at http://www.holytrinitymission.org/books/english/russian_spirituality_fedotov.htm (March 4, 2008).

38 Vsévolod Rochcau, *Saint Séraphim, Sarov et Divéyevo: études et documents, suivis d'une étude sur un fragment inédit des Récits d'un pèlerin russse* (Bégrolles-en-Mauges: Abbaye de Bellefontaine, 1987).

39 Valerie Zander, *St. Seraphim of Sarov*, translated by Sister Gabriel Anne and introduced by Father. Boris Bobrinskoy (London: The Society for Promoting Christian Knowledge, 1975).

40 Benedict Nightingale, "Greek Islands to Call Home," *New York Times*, September 28, 1997.

41 John Freely, *The Cyclades: Discovering the Greek Islands of the Aegean* (London: I.B. Tauris, 2006), 96.

42 Constantine Cavarnos, *St. Arsenios of Paros: Remarkable Confessor, Spiritual Guide, Educator, Ascetic, Miracle-worker, and Healer; An Account of His Life, Character, Message and Miracles* (Belmont, MA: Institute for Byzantine and Modern Greek Studies, 1978).

43 Archimandrite Philotheos Zervakos, *The Life, Conduct, and Miracles of Our Father Arsenios the New, Who Led a Life of Spiritual Endeavor on the Island of Paros* (Athens, 1960; 2nd ed. 1976).

44 Constantine Cavarnos, *St. Arsenios of Paros: Remarkable Confessor, Spiritual Guide, Educator, Ascetic, Miracle-worker, and Healer; An Account of His Life, Character, Message and Miracles* (Belmont, MA: Institute for Byzantine and Modern Greek Studies, 1978), 27.

45 Theophanis the Monk, "The Ladder of Divine Graces," in *The Philokalia: The Complete Text; Compiled by St. Nikodemus of the Holy Mountain and St. Makarius of Corinth.* Translated and edited

by G.E.H. Palmer, Philip Sherrard, and Kallistos Ware, 4 vols. (London: Faber and Faber Limited, 1979-1995), 3:67.

46 Constantine Cavarnos, *St. Arsenios of Paros: Remarkable Confessor, Spiritual Guide, Educator, Ascetic, Miracle-worker, and Healer; An Account of His Life, Character, Message and Miracles* (Belmont, MA: Institute for Byzantine and Modern Greek Studies, 1978), 31.
47 Ibid., 73.
48 Ibid., 80.
49 Ibid., 81-83.
50 Ibid., 83.
51 Ibid., 83-84.
52 Ibid., 84-85.
53 Ibid., 85-86.
54 Ibid., 86-87.
55 Ibid., 87-88.
56 Ibid., 88-89.
57 Ibid., 89-92.
58 Ibid., 93-94.
59 Ibid., 94-96.
60 Ibid., 96-98.
61 Ibid., 98-101.
62 Ibid., 101.

CHAPTER SEVEN

Miracles on Mt. Athos

If any man will come after me, let him deny himself, and take up his cross, and follow me.
For whosoever will save his life shall lose it: and whosoever will lose his life for my sake shall find it.

—Mat 16:24-25

Mt. Athos is located on the easternmost of three promontories which project from the Chalcidice (also spelled Halkidiki) peninsula in northern Greece (the Macedonian province) into the Aegean Sea. Athos is 30 miles long and 6.5 miles wide at its broadest point. Although it is connected to land, access by sea alone is permitted.

According to athonite tradition, Mary, the Mother of Christ, accompanied by St. John the Evangelist, left Joppa and sailed to Cyprus to visit Lazarus.[1] En route, Mary's vessel was blown off course and she was forced to anchor on Mt. Athos near the port of Klement, in the vicinity where the monastery of Iviron now stands.

Mary was delighted by the rare beauty of the peninsula and prayed to her Son to give it to her as a gift. A voice came from the sky saying, "Let this place be your inheritance and your garden, a paradise and a haven of salvation for those seeking to be saved." Since then Athos has been consecrated to the Virgin Mary and has come to be known as "the Garden of the Mother of God." Today there are 20 monasteries on Athos: 17 Greek, one Russian, one Serbian, and one Bulgarian; there are also a number of monk-huts (*skiti*) on Athos.

The monks on Athos have surrendered everything to follow Christ and they live a very disciplined lifestyle of rigorous fasting and continual prayer. For example, they are awakened from their sleep at 11 PM by the sound of the *symantron* (a long wooden cymbal) for an hour of private prayer. The monks recite "Lord Jesus Christ, have mercy on me" on the rosary and then return to sleep until 4 AM when they are awakened once more by the sound of the *symantron*. They attend church for matins, the chanting of the hours, and liturgy. Liturgy lasts until 10:30 AM. Then they eat the main meal of the day and attend to their tasks afterwards. Having completed their duties, they attend church services again, either at 3 PM or at 5 PM, depending on the time of the year. Supper is at 7 PM and afterwards they retire until 11 PM when they are awakened by the *symantron* once more. Sometimes vigils are held that require attendance throughout the evening, night, and the following morning.

Athos has produced a formidable number of patriarchs, archbishops, bishops, saints, ascetics, and men of prayer. The Great Lavra, the oldest of the 20 monasteries on Mt. Athos, has by itself produced 36 patriarchs and more than 144 bishops.

Athos is the site of a wealth of rare and unique treasures dating back to the time of Christ. Its monasteries house the largest piece of the True Cross, the three boxes that held the frankincense, gold, and myrrh that the three Magi presented to the Infant Jesus, ancient icons that perform miracles, adorned in gold, silver, and precious jewels, the remains of saints, libraries of rare ancient texts, and invaluable gifts given by Byzantine emperors. There are more than 18,000 icons on Athos dating back to the 10th century and they have a history of performing miracles.

We recommend the following books on Mt. Athos: Anthony Bryer and Mary Cunningham, eds., *Mount Athos and Byzantine Monasticism: Papers from the Twenty-eighth Spring Symposium of Byzantine Studies, Birmingham, March 1994*;[2] Robert Byron, *The Station Athos: Treasures and Men*;[3] Richard McGillvray Dawkins, *The Monks of Mount Athos*;[4] Frederick William Hasluck, *Athos and its Monasteries*;[5] Chris Hellier, *Monasteries of Greece*;[6] *The Holy and Great Monastery of Vatopaidi: Tradition, History, Art*;[7] William M. Johnston, ed., *Encyclopedia of Monasticism*;[8] Sotiris Kada, *Mount Athos: An Illustrated Guide to the Monasteries and their History*;[9] Christopher Merrill, *Things of the Hidden God: Journey to the Holy Mountain*;[10] John Julius Norwich and Reresby Sitwell, *Mount Athos*;[11] Giota Oikonomake-Papadopoulou, *Enkolpia: The Holy and Great Monastery of Vatopaidi*;[12] Stelios Papadopoulos, *The Holy Xenophontos Monastery: The Icons*;[13] Stelios Papadopoulos, ed., *Simonopetra, Mount Athos*;[14] Stelios Papadopoulos and Chrysoula Kapioldassi-Soteropoulou, eds., *Icons of the Holy Monastery of Pantokrator*;[15] Philip Sherrard, *Athos: The Holy Mountain*;[16] Philip Sherrard, *Athos, the Mountain of Silence*;[17] Ploutarchos Theocharides, Pandelis Foundas, Stergios Stefanou, *Mount Athos*;[18] Timothy Ware, *The Orthodox Church*.[19]

THE MIRACULOUS ICON OF AXION ESTI

On June 11, 980 AD a company of monks were holding an all-night vigil at the Holy Dormition Cathedral in Karyes, Mt. Athos. They sang a hymn to the Virgin Mary written by St. Cosmas in 720 AD. St. Cosmas is considered to be one of the great hymnographers of Orthodoxy. The hymn was called "Axion Esti," meaning "it is truly meet," "it is truly proper." The monks began the hymn thus: "More worthy of honor than the cherubim; and beyond compare more glorious than the seraphim. You, who incorruptibly gave birth to God the Word, verily Theotokos we extol you."

During their vigil the monks noticed a man whom they had never seen before dressed in the habit of a monk. They did not know who he was, nor could they explain his sudden appearance from nowhere. This new monk began to chant "Axion Esti" in a beautiful voice, but added the following verse to the beginning of the hymn: "It is meet and right to bless you, ever-esteemed Theotokos [God-bearer], most pure and Mother of our God." The monk instructed the group that the angelic choirs in Heaven preface the hymn with these additional words. Then the monk identified himself: he was the Archangel Gabriel and he instructed the monks to add these words to the hymn. Then the Archangel vanished before them, leaving them amazed at the power of God. Since that day, June 11, 980 AD, Axion Esti has been chanted in the new version according to Gabriel's instructions by Orthodox Christians throughout the world.

THE MIRACULOUS PORTATISSA ICON
AT THE IVIRON MONASTERY

One of the most venerated icons on Mount Athos is called the Portatissa Icon. According to tradition, a widow in Nicea had the icon in her possession for safe keeping. However, an unbelieving

Roman soldier struck it with his sword with the intention of destroying it. Upon impact, the face of the icon began to gush blood. The Roman soldier, astounded by the miracle, believed and converted to Christianity.

In order to protect the icon from further destruction, the widow placed the icon in the sea and left it to God to direct its path henceforth. Eventually the icon was beached on the shores of the promontory of Mount Athos near the Georgian Iviron Monastery.

Then another miracle occurred: no matter how many times the monks brought the icon indoors, the icon was always found at the gate of the monastery. Thus, it received the name Portatissa (All Holy of the Gate or She Who Guards the Gate) and the monks built a chapel at the entrance to the monastery. Today the miraculous icon continues to be venerated at Iviron's gate and its discovery on the beach is commemorated with an annual procession to the shore.

Graham Speake, in *Mount Athos: Renewal in Paradise*, describes the Miracle of the Portatissa Icon thus:

> …the hermit monk Gabriel…took it from the sea and placed it in the *katholikon* (that is, the main church) of the monastery, only to find next day that it had removed itself to a spot over the old entrance gate of the monastery. They took it back to the church, and again it repositioned itself over the gate. This happened three times, after which the Virgin appeared in a vision to Fr Gabriel and told him that a special chapel should be built for the icon next to the gate, "for I have not come here for you to guard me, but for me to guard you." The chapel was duly built and to this day it houses the icon, that is therefore known as Our Lady of the Gate.[20]

THE MIRACULOUS ICON TRICHEROUSA
AT CHILANDAR MONASTERY

Speake also discusses the events surrounding another miraculous icon, one that depicts Mary with three hands. This icon moved by itself to the abbot's chair in Chilandar Monastery. Mary appeared in a vision to one of the monks there telling him that it was her intention to place the icon in the abbot's chair in order to settle a dispute among the monks:

> Another icon of the Mother of God said to date from the period of iconoclasm is the so-called Tricherousa, or Our Lady with Three Hands, at the monastery of Chilandar… This icon apparently belonged to the eighth-century theologian St John of Damascus, whose hand was cut off by the Caliph when he mistakenly thought John was plotting against him. The mistake was discovered and the hand restored, in gratitude for which John had a silver hand attached to the icon. In the twelfth century the Tricherousa was given to St Savvas, archbishop of Serbia and co-founder (with his father Stefan Nemanya) of the monastery of Chilandar, though the icon itself did not reach Athos until 1371. As at Iviron, the monks placed it in the chancel of the katholikon, where it remained until a dispute occurred over the election of a new abbot. Then one morning the monks noticed that the icon had repositioned itself over the abbot's throne. They put it back in the chancel, and again it removed itself to the throne. This happened three times, after which a hermit told the monks that the Mother of God had appeared to him in a vision and told him that this was her way of settling the dispute. From now on she would take the role of abbot and the monks should elect only a deputy abbot. And to this day the abbot's throne is occupied by the Tricherousa.[21]

THE MIRACLE-WORKING GIRDLE OF MARY AT VATOPEDI MONASTERY

Among the many invaluable treasures dating to the time of Christ that Mount Athos holds, is the girdle [*zoni* in Greek] that Mary wore. Historically, this precious artifact has worked many miracles. Speake discusses the girdle of the Virgin Mary that she gave to the apostle Thomas at the time of her Assumption into Heaven. Speake takes care to point out that among the miracles that the *zoni* has performed is the restoration of fertility to barren women:

> And the most cherished sacred treasure at the monastery of Vatopedi is…the girdle of the Mother of God, which is the only surviving relic of her earthly life. Now in three pieces, it is made of camel's hair, supposedly fashioned by the Virgin herself. At her Assumption she gave it to St. Thomas and it remained in Jerusalem until the fourth century, when the emperor Arcadius removed it to Constantinople. Always prized as an agent of healing, it cured the empress Zoë, wife of Leo VI, and in gratitude she embroidered it with the gold thread that still adorns it today…Over the years it has performed many miracles, particularly in the case of barren women, and it is still occasionally taken out into the world to heal the faithful.[22]

In addition, Vatopedi Monastery possesses eight miraculous healing icons of Mary and other monasteries on Mount Athos also have miracle-working icons of the Blessed Mother. The eight icons at Vatopedi Monastery are named Queen of the Altar (also known as Vimatarissa or Ktitorissa), Comfort or Consolation (Paramythia), Slain (Esphagmeni), Responsive (Antiphonitria), Merciful or Compassionate (Eleousa), She Who flows with Oil (Elaiovrytissa), She Who was Shot (Pyrovolitheisa), and

Queen of All (Pantanassa). In addition, the Monastery at Karyes has It is Meet (Axion Esti); the Monastery of Great Lavra has Koukouzelissa, an icon of Mary named after St. John Koukouzelis, who was Great Lavra's hymnographer, master of music, theorist and composer, and another icon named Stewardess (Economissa) ; Koutloumousiou Monastery has Awe-inspiring Protection (Phoveraprostasia); Pantokrator has the Holy Elder (Gerontissa, which is the feminine form of elder); Philotheou Monastery has the One of the Sweet Kiss (Glykophilousa) and another Gerontissa (Holy Elder); Dochiariou Monastery has She Who is Quick to Hear or She Who Answers Prayers Quickly (Gorgoypekoös); Dionysiou Monastery has Full of Fragrance (Myrovlitissa); Zografu Monastery has Listening (Epakouousa).

TWO MIRACLES SURROUNDING THE REBUILDING OF THE VATOPEDI MONASTERY

The monastery at Vatopedi has been destroyed and rebuilt several times during its tempestuous history. Speake recounts that there are two great miracles surrounding its rebuilding. In fact, the monastery derives its name from one of these miracles.[23] The Emperor Constantine the Great, who reigned over the Byzantine Empire during 324-37 AD, founded the monastery; subsequently, Julian the Apostate (360-63) destroyed it. Then Theodosius the Great (379-95) rebuilt it to give thanks to the Virgin Mary for miraculously saving his infant son during a shipwreck. The baby, named Arcadius, who was tossed off the ship, miraculously survived the tempestuous waters and was safely deposited in a bramble bush on the shore by the Blessed Virgin. Theodosius, in gratitude to the Mother of God for mercifully protecting his child from death, built a monastery at the very site on which the child was found, naming it Vatodpedi: *vatos* means bramble bush; *paidi*, child.

Speake goes on to discuss another miracle, even more striking than the first, that occurred at Vatopedi. Although Theodosius rebuilt the monastery in the 4th century, it was destroyed once more by Syrian pirates in the 10th century. During the pirates' siege, the sacristan (*vimataris*) rushed to hide a precious irreplaceable treasure that the monastery housed: the Cross of Constantine. This sacristan, whose name was Savvas, was led by the Holy Spirit to hide the Cross in a well. Reaching into the well, Savvas placed the Cross next to an icon of Mary and then set a burning candlestick by these two objects. Unfortunately, Savvas was captured and taken to Crete as a prisoner. It was not until 70 years had passed that Crete was liberated (961) and that Savvas was able to return to Vatopedi. Upon his arrival, he had the monks open the well and it was then that all present witnessed the great miracle that had transpired: the Cross was there, the icon of Mary was standing by it, upright in the water, and the candle was still burning brightly after 70 years! Today this well is situated beneath the sanctuary of the katholikon; the Cross is on the altar; and the miraculous icon, named the *Vimatarissa* (Virgin of the Sacristan), with the eternal candlestick burning next to it, protect and keep watch over the altar of Vatopedi.[24]

Endnotes

1   The Lord did not want His mother to remain alone after His mission was completed. On the Cross He entrusted her to the apostle John, who was to become her adoptive son: "When Jesus therefore saw his mother, and the disciple standing by, whom he loved, he saith unto his mother, Woman, behold they son! Then saith he to the disciple, Behold thy mother! And from that hour that disciple took her unto his own home" (John 19:26-27). Also, after the Lord resurrected Lazarus, he founded a church in Kition (now Larnaca, Cyprus), where he became bishop.

2   Anthony Bryer and Mary Cunningham, eds., *Mount Athos and Byzantine Monasticism: Papers from the Twenty-eighth Spring Symposium of Byzantine Studies, Birmingham, March 1994* (Brookfield, VT: Variorum, 1996).

3   Robert Byron, *The Station Athos: Treasures and Men* (London: Duckworth, 1928).

4   Richard McGillivray Dawkins, *The Monks of Mount Athos* (London: G. Allen & Unwin, Ltd, 1936).

5   Frederick William Hasluck, *Athos and its Monasteries* (London: K. Paul, Trench, Trubner & Co. Ltd, 1924).

6   Chris Hellier, *Monasteries of Greece* (London: Tauris Parke, 1996).

7   *The Holy and Great Monastery of Vatopaidi: Tradition, History, Art* (Mount Athos: The Monastery, 1998).

8   William M. Johnston, ed., *Encyclopedia of Monasticism*, 2 vols. (Chicago: Fitzroy Dearborn, 2000).

9   Sotiris Kadas, *Mount Athos: An Illustrated Guide to the Monasteries and their History* (Athens: Ekdotike Athenon, 1980).

10   Christopher Merrill, *Things of the Hidden God: Journey to the Holy Mountain* (New York: Random House, 2005).

11   John Julius Norwich and Reresby Sitwell, *Mount Athos* (London: Hutchinson, 1966).

12   Giota Oikonomake-Papadopoulou, *Enkolpia: The Holy and Great Monastery of Vatopaidi* Mount Athos: The Holy and Great Monastery of Vatopaidi, 2001).

13   Stelios Papadopoulos, *The Holy Xenophontos Monastery: The Icons* (Mount Athos: The Holy Xenophontos Monastery, 1999).

14   Stelios Papadopoulos, ed., *Simonopetra, Mount Athos* (Athens: ETBA, Hellenic Industrial Development Bank SA, 1991).

15   Stelios Papadopoulos and Chrysoula Kapioldassi-Soteropoulou, eds., *Icons of the Holy Monastery of Pantokrator* (Mount Athos: Pantokrator Holy Monastery, 1998).

16   Philip Sherrard, *Athos: The Holy Mountain*, photographs by Takis Zervoulakos (London: Sidgwick & Jackson, 1982).

17   Philip Sherrard, *Athos, the Mountain of Silence* (London: Oxford University Press, 1960).

18   Ploutarchos Theocharides, Pandelis Foundas, Stergios Stefanou, *Mount Athos*, translated by Philip Ramp (Athens: Melissa Publishing House, 1992).

19   Timothy Ware, *The Orthodox Church*, rev. ed. (London: Penguin Books, 1997), 38-39, 79, 92, 99-101, 107, 117, 129-32, 136, 187, 191, 273.

20   Graham Speake, *Mount Athos: Renewal in Paradise* (New Haven: Yale University Press, 2002), 21.

21   Ibid., 21-22.

22   Ibid., 22-24.

23   Ibid., 27.

24   Ibid., 28.

CHAPTER EIGHT

Miracles Authenticated by the Orthodox Church in the News

...upon this rock I will build my church; and the gates of hell shall not prevail against it. And I will give unto thee the keys of the kingdom of heaven: and whatsoever thou shalt bind on earth shall be bound in heaven: and whatsoever thou shalt loose on earth shall be loosed in heaven.

—Mat 16:18-19

WHY GOD USES ICONS TO PERFORM MIRACLES

God performs modern day miracles, as He has done in the past, through holy icons. The press has given considerable coverage to occasions when icons that depict Mary holding the Infant Jesus have begun to cry, when holy oil gushes forth from icons, and when icons that touch miraculous icons also begin to perform miracles. Since God uses holy icons as instruments to perform His will, let us examine why this is so.

Historically, God has often used icons as vehicles to commune with man, as means of celebration, as instruments by which He may be glorified, and as a way to show that He is very near. That is why icons have an important role in Orthodox liturgy, the worship of the Risen Lord, and the veneration of the saints. In the Orthodox Church they are regarded as windows to Heaven, as doorways of communication between man and the Living God and sometimes God uses them as instruments through which He performs miracles of healing in response to the prayers of the faithful. In order to understand why this is so, it is necessary to begin by addressing the dual nature of man and God's plan for man's eventual theosis or deification. It is man in his deified state that icons capture and convey. It is precisely because icons portray the saints' glorified state, reveal our own future deified state, and are regarded as windows into God's timeless Kingdom, that God uses them to communicate with man through miracles and signs.

THE SON OF GOD BECAME MAN SO THAT MEN MIGHT BECOME THE SONS OF GOD

Man is comprised of two elements, body and spirit. The Eternal God, on the other hand, was spirit only before He came to earth to redeem us. However, that changed when He journeyed to earth to tabernacle among us. The apostle John begins his gospel by declaring that God chose to come to earth and be clothed in human flesh so that we might become the sons of God: "In the beginning was the Word, and the Word was with God, and the Word was God. The same was in the beginning with God...He was in the world, and the world was made by him, and the world knew him not. He came unto his own, and his own received him not. But as many as received him, to them gave he power to become the sons of God, even to them that believe on his name" (John 1:1-2, 10-12).

That humans are the sons of God is revealed in the OT: "I have said, Ye are gods; and all of you are children of the most High" (Ps 82:6). Despite the fact that men are gods, they must die in the flesh, and the next verse reads, "But ye shall die like men, and fall like one of the princes" (Ps 82:7).

Christ reiterates the fact that men are gods in his response to those who attempted to stone Him: "Jesus answered them, Is it not written in your law, I said, Ye are gods? If he called them gods, unto whom the word of God came, and the scripture cannot be broken; Say ye of him, whom the Father hath sanctified, and sent into the world, Thou blasphemest; because I said, I am the Son of God?" (John 10:34-36). Here Christ reminds men that the statement made in Ps 82:6 is, indeed, a fact; that it is the Word of God that has come to men; and that scripture cannot be broken, its truths are eternal. "If he called them gods, unto whom the word of God came" is true on two levels. First, the psalmist who uttered Ps 82:6 was speaking to Israel, and his words were those that were given to him by the Holy Spirit. The psalmist is relaying the word of God to his people. Secondly, the Word of God is Christ, He is the One who has come to men; He was speaking of Himself when He said, "If he called them gods, unto whom the word of God came."

Christ's statements that the Father has sanctified Him and sent Him into the world (John 10:36), and "I am the Son of God" (John 10:36) are not only reiterated, but developed by the apostle Peter. Peter gives us the logical corollary to Christ's teaching. Peter instructs us that Christ has called us to share in His shining greatness and perfect life, which hold great and exceeding promises; it is by these great and exceeding promises "that…ye might become partakers of the divine nature" (2 Pet 1:4).

Irenaeus, the Bishop of Lugdunum (Lyon) in Gaul, teaches us that the Son of God became man so that men might become the sons of God through adoption. In *Irenaeus against Hereses* [*Contra hæreses*] (c. 180 AD), he advises, "For it was for this end that the Word of God was made man, and He who was the Son of God became the Son of man, that man, having been taken into the Word, and receiving the adoption, might become the son of God. For by no other means could we have attained to incorruptibility and immortality, unless we had been united to incorruptibility and immortality. But how could we be joined to incorruptibility and immortality, unless, first, incorruptibility and immortality had become that which we also are, so that the corruptible might be swallowed up by incorruptibility, and the mortal by immortality, that we might receive the adoption of sons?"[1] Irenaeus is teaching that it is our divine adoption that is the source of our deification.

Athanasius, Patriarch of Alexandria, in *On the Incarnation of the Word of God* [*Oratio de Incarnatione Verbi*], 54.3, affirms, "For he was made man that we might be made God; and he manifested Himself by a body that we might receive the idea of the unseen Father; and He endured the insolence of men that we might inherit immortality."[2]

The Church Fathers teach that Christ became man so that man might be deified in the following works: Irenaeus, in *Irenaeus against Heresies* [*Contra hæreses*], 3.17-19;[3] Athanasius, in *Against the Arians* [*Oratio II contra Arianos*], 2.59;[4] Cyril of Alexandria, *Commentary on the Gospel according to S. John* [*In Joannis Evangelium Lib. I*], John 1:13-14;[5] John Chrysostom, *Homilies on the Gospel of St. John* [*In Joannem homiliæ*], John 1:14;[6] Peter Chrysologus, *Sermons on the Lord's Prayer* [*Sermones in orationem Dominicam*], 67, 68.3, 70, 71.2-3, 72.3.[7]

Daniel B. Clendenin, in *Eastern Orthodox Christianity: A Western Perspective*, summarizes the teachings of the early fathers thus: "Both Macarius of Egypt and Chrysostom interpret the marriage analogy in 1 Cor 6:17 as referring to our spiritual marriage in which 'the soul is united to God in an ineffable union.'[8] According to Ilias the Presbyter (c. 110), it is when we attain divine likeness through theosis that we transcend the differences between male and female (Gal 3:28).[9] We are, writes the apostle Paul, 'created to be like God' and 'imitators of God' (Eph 4:24; 5:1)."[10]

THE LORD'S TRANSFIGURATION ON MOUNT TABOR WAS A FORESHADOWING OF MAN'S THEOSIS

When Christ came to earth, He did not give up His divine nature. This fact is seen in His glorious Transfiguration on Mount Tabor (Mat 17:1-9; Mark 9:2-9; Luke 9:28-36). Three apostles, Peter, James, and John, saw the Glorified Christ, whose body and clothing were consumed by divine illumination, conversing with Moses and Elijah. The Transfigured Lord is described thus: "And was transfigured before them: and his face did shine as the sun, and his raiment was white as the light" (Mat 17:2); "...he was transfigured before them. And his raiment became shining, exceeding white as snow; so as no fuller on earth can white them" (Mark 9:2-3); "And as he prayed, the fashion of his countenance was altered, and his raiment was white and glistering" (Luke 9:29).

Iconographer and iconologist Leonid Ouspensky, in *Theology of the Icon*, explains that the Lord's Transfiguration shows us what awaits us in Heaven when we achieve theosis:

> The future transfiguration of the entire human race, including that of the body, is prefigured for us in the transfiguration of the Lord on Mount Tabor...The

Lord no longer appeared to his disciples in his "form of a servant," but as God. The whole body of Christ was transfigured, becoming, so to speak, the luminous clothing of his divinity. In his transfiguration "on Mount Tabor, not only divinity appeared to men, but humanity also appeared in divine glory."[11] The fathers of the seventh ecumenical council explain: "With regard to the nature of the transfiguration, it took place not in such a way that the Word left the human image, but rather in the illumination of this human image by his glory..."[12]

According to the Fathers, Christ showed to his disciples the deified state to which all are called. Just as the body of our Lord was glorified and transfigured, becoming resplendent with the divine glory and infinite light, so also the bodies of saints are glorified and become luminous, being transfigured by the force of divine grace. Seraphim of Sarov not only explained, but directly and visibly revealed this likeness between man and God by transfiguring himself before the eyes of his disciple Nicholas Motovilov...[13]

Grace penetrates human nature, is united with it, and from this point on one begins to live the life of the world to come. This is why we can say that a saint is more fully human than the sinner is. Saints are free from sin, which is essentially foreign to human nature; they realize the primordial meaning of their existence; with their lives they participate in constructing and put on the incorruptible beauty of the kingdom of God. For this reason beauty, as it is understood by the Orthodox Church, is not the characteristic beauty of a creature. It is a part of the life to come, when God will be all in all...true beauty is the radiance of the Holy Spirit, the holiness of and participation in the life of the world to come.[14]

The definition of theosis is divinizatin or union with the Living God. The Orthodox Church teaches that Scripture indicates that this is exactly what the purpose of man is: union with the Living God. *The Philokalia* declares that the way to achieve theosis may be metaphorized as a ladder to God. Christians embark on a journey. The first step on the ladder is faith. Once they believe, they begin a journey on which they become more and more like Christ.

ICONS DEPICT THE SAINTS WHO HAVE ACHIEVED THEOSIS

It is this glorified state of Christ, Mary, and the saints, all of whom have achieved theosis, that Orthodox icons capture. The icons of the East do not only depict the physical nature of the saints as do the icons of the West: they also depict the spiritual nature. This is done using various techniques. For example, there is a circle of light behind the head that conveys the light emanating from the saint in the deified state that he has achieved.

In icons depicting Mary, her eyes are directed inward, gazing into the spiritual realm, looking beyond the physical world. Holding the Infant Christ, Mary is contemplating the words of the angel Gabriel when he announced, "Fear not, Mary: for thou hast found favour with God. And, behold, thou shall conceive in thy womb, and bring forth a son, and shalt call his name JESUS. He shall be great, and shall be called the Son of the Highest: and the Lord God shall give unto him the throne of his father David: And he shall reign over the house of Jacob for ever: and of his kingdom there shall be no end…The Holy Ghost shall come upon thee and the power of the Highest shall overshadow thee: therefore also that holy thing which shall be born of thee shall be called the Son of God" (Luke 1:30-33, 35). Icons depict Mary's contemplation of God's mystery that the angel had announced in a manner that it is evident to the onlooker. An illiterate can understand the spiritual truths without reading: the Virgin's eyes are turned inwards and her mind is contemplating the angel's great and exceeding promises. She is holding her newborn baby in her arms. The angel foretold that she would give birth to the Son of God. His conception was miraculous. She is filled with wonder and awe at the power of Almighty God.

We also see Mary's great humility and readiness to conform her will to God's will when we see her icon. Her response to Gabriel's Annunciation was, "Behold the handmaid of the Lord; be it unto me according to thy word" (Luke 1:38). She professes her faith, her love of God, and her obedience to His will to her cousin, Elizabeth: "My soul doth magnify the Lord, And my spirit hath rejoiced in God my Saviour. For he hath regarded the low estate of his handmaiden: for, behold, from henceforth all generations shall call me blessed. For he that is mighty hath done to me great things; and holy is his name. And his mercy is on them that fear him from generation to generation. He hath shewed strength with his arm; he hath scattered the proud in the imagination of their hearts. He hath put down the mighty from their seats, and exalted them of low degree. He hath filled the hungry with good things; and the rich he hath sent empty away" (Luke 1:46-53). Because the icon depicts the soul of the person, icons of Mary capture what we know about her from these biblical passages: that her heart is brimming with the love of God; that she has great humility before God; that she is grateful that He has chosen her to carry out His will on earth; that she praises and glorifies God in her thoughts, words, and deeds. Mary knows God and she declares His mercy and justice: she professes God's great mercy on those who fear Him through all generations; she declares that He is a just God who metes out justice to nations and individuals who turn away from Him, that He shows His strength; that He fills the hungry (poor in spirit), while turning away those who value money and power more than Him. Her faithfulness to God is one among countless reasons that he has chosen her to be the vehicle through which He would accomplish His mission on earth. Mary's humility, Christ-like nature, readiness to obey God, are all evident to the onlooker who gazes at her icon. He does not have to guess at or infer her Christ-like nature. It is plain for all to see.

Iconographers depict Mary holding Jesus to remind us of the special relationship that God has with this mortal who was willing to be the vehicle through which His will would be accomplished. However, her deified nature permeates her icons, and the onlooker knows that he is regarding the Mother of God in her deified, glorified state. A heavenly, God-given peace permeates her soul and surrounds her form. Peace, although it is a state of being and not an object, is captured and depicted in a holy icon. Peace, the hallmark of God's Eternal Kingdom, fills the onlooker at he gazes at the icon.

Mary has reached human potential, union with God, something that awaits every believer. When we gaze at the icon of Mary, we see our future state. We gaze into the heavenly realm and experience its peace. Mary and Christ are alive in Heaven. The saints are alive in the presence of the Lord. The interior of the Orthodox Church, covered with icons, gives a warm feeling to the visitor, like a sip of brandy. That is because Heaven is a warm place to be-a place where we will be reunited with our loved ones who, too, are awaiting the reunion. The colorful icons that surround us remind us that we are never alone-the spiritual realm is far reaching and everlasting; God is a God of the living, not the dead. Christ has kept His promise: believers who are absent in the flesh are present with the Lord (2 Cor 5:1-8). One outward sign or evidence that this spiritual realm exists and is very, very near, is miracles, as we shall see.

The function of the icon is to capture the divine nature of the saint as well as his humanity. An example of this fact is seen in

Saint Seraphim of Sarov, who assumed a form of bright light before his disciple, Nicholas Motovilov: the saint resembled Christ during His Transformation on Mount Tabor. It is truly miraculous that the saint was seen in his glorified form (a form that we, too, will one day have) while he was still alive in the flesh. Iconographers of Saint Seraphim depict his transfiguration: they portray a human who is divinely transfigured and a deified person who has human qualities. Leonid Ouspensky explains the dual objective of the iconographer thus:

> ...the icon is an image not only of a living but also of a deified prototype. It does not represent the corruptible flesh destined for decomposition, but transfigured flesh illuminated by grace, the flesh of the world to come (see 1 Cor 15:35-46). It portrays the divine beauty and glory in material ways which are visible to physical eyes. The icon is venerable and holy precisely because it portrays this deified state of its prototype and bears his name. This is why grace, characteristic of the prototype, is present in the icon. In other words, the grace of the Holy Spirit sustains the holiness both of the represented person and of his icon, and this grace brings about the relationship between the faithful and the saint through the intermediary of the icon of the saint. The icon participates in the holiness of its prototype and through the icon, we in turn participate in this holiness in our prayers.[15]

Ouspensky points out that an icon and a portrait are two different things, having two different functions. The difference between an icon and a portrait was articulated by the seventh ecumenical council: a portrait depicts only the mortal, corruptible man; the icon shows the man who has achieved his divine state; the icon shows both natures-the physical and the deified. Unlike the portrait, the icon depicts the glorified, future state of humanity that was displayed by the Lord on Mount Tabor. The icon makes this evident to the onlooker so that he does not have to guess at its meaning.[16]

Icons have a significant role in Orthodox liturgy and worship because they remind us that the saints have achieved theosis. It is precisely because these men and women of God have done so, that they have the ability to hear the prayers of the faithful around the world and answer them. Icons, which capture the physical and the spiritual nature of the saints that they portray, are regarded as doors of communication between the earthly and the Heavenly realms. God must think so, too, because He uses them as instruments by which He is glorified and Christ's triumphant Resurrection is celebrated. He has utilized them throughout the centuries to perform miracles: these miracles strengthen people's faith, heal the sick and suffering, and communicate His faithfulness and the fact that He is near and ever present. Therefore, it is understandable why icons have been given prominence in Orthodoxy.

Because icons are windows to heaven, they are displayed prominently in the Orthodox Church. They cover the solid screen or wall that divides the sanctuary from the rest of the church. This wall is called the iconostasis and it is covered with icons. Icons are also placed around the church in their own special shrines. They are part of the liturgy: priests direct incense towards them with their censors, parishioners prostrate themselves before them and kiss them to honor the saints that they depict. They continually remind us of the life to come-that the saints are not dead, but rather, that they are alive and in the presence of God; that the saints have achieved theosis or union with God; that the saints answer prayers, perform miracles of healing, and that they often reveal their sanctity and the fact that they have achieved the deified state, by leaving behind incorruptible relics that survive the centuries, relics that often smell of frankincense, myrrh and sweet perfume, as signs. They remind us that God is not a God of the dead, but of the living.

Leontius, Bishop of Neapolis (modern Limassol, Cyprus) (7th century), explains the veneration of icons thus:

> We do not adore as gods the figures and images of the saints. For if it was the mere wood of the image that we adored as God, we should likewise adore all wood, and not, as often happens, when the form grows faint, throw the image into the fire. And again, as long as the wood remains in the form of a cross, I adore it on account of Christ who was crucified upon it. When it falls to pieces, I throw them into the fire. just as the man who receives the sealed orders of the king and embraces the seal, looks upon the dust and paper and wax as honourable in their reference to the king's service, so we Christians, in worshipping the Cross, do not worship the wood for itself, but seeing in it the impress and seal and figure of Christ Himself, crucified through it and on it, we fall down and adore.[17]

Icons are teaching tools: they are useful for instruction. If we want to explain Christianity to an unbeliever, and if he is illiterate and cannot read the Bible or biographies of the saints, all one has to do is take him to a church and show him the icons. He can see the life and landmark events in the mission of Christ on earth, the lives of the saints, what their legacies are. Hence, they are useful in teaching about God and how His people martyred themselves for Him because they believed. Early Christians saw the Risen Lord, believed, and were willing to become martyrs for the Immortal, Incorruptible Lord because they had seen Him. Leontius says that icons are opened books that remind us of God:

They are not our gods, but books which lie open and are venerated in churches in order to remind us of God and to lead us to worship Him. He who honours the martyr honours God, to whom the martyr bore testimony.[18]

Icons are textbooks that transcend the thousands of languages that exist on earth; without words, they teach the historicity of Christ, of His mission on earth, and the miracles that have continued throughout the centuries during the Church age since Pentecost.

John of Damascus advises that we are permitted to make icons precisely because God came to earth and took the form of man. He journeyed to the physical realm, took on physical form, and walked among us. Therefore, when we make icons depicting Christ, we have a picture in our minds of a historical event, but more than that, of the God who tabernacled among us. In *On the Divine Images: Three Apologies against Those Who Attack the Divine Images* (c. 730), John of Damascus reiterates the gospel of John the Apostle, "In the beginning was the Word, and the Word was with God, and the Word was God. The same was in the beginning with God…He was in the world, and the world was made by him, and the world knew him not. He came unto his own, and his own received him not. But as many as received him, to them gave he power to become the sons of God, even to them that believe on his name" (John 1:1-2, 10-12). The Creator of the universe chose to visit us and assume physical form. Therefore, we, His created beings, are justified in drawing pictures of Him to honor Him and to celebrate His Resurrection and Glory. What better way to declare the Resurrected, Eternal Son of God to the world than to paint beautiful pictures of Him?

John of Damascus declares:

> Of old, God the incorporeal and uncircumscribed was never depicted. Now, however, when God is seen clothed in flesh, and conversing with men, (Bar. 3.38) I make an image of the God whom I see. I do not worship matter, I worship the God of matter, who became matter for my sake, and deigned to inhabit matter, who worked out my salvation through matter. I will not cease from honouring that matter which works my salvation.[19]

It is precisely because icons are a glorification of God, a celebration of Christ's victory on the Cross on behalf of humanity, of the triumph of good over evil, that God uses icons to perform miracles of healing. Patriarch Diodorus I has said that when God performs miracles, He reminds us that Heaven is very near. When people are committed to Christ, Christ pours forth miracles for His Bride, the Church.

Excellent books that explain the role of icons in Orthodox worship include: John Baggley, *Doors of Perception-Icons and their Spiritual Significance*;[20] Daniel B. Clendenin, *Eastern Orthodox Christianity: A Western Perspective*;[21] Daniel B. Clendenin, *Eastern Orthodox Theology: A Contemporary Reader*;[22] Paul Evdokimov, *The Art of the Icon: A Theology of Beauty*;[23] St. John of Damascus, *On the Divine Images: Three Apologies against Those Who Attack the Divine Images*;[24] Leonid Ouspensky, *Theology of the Icon*;[25] Leonid Ouspensky and Vladimir Lossky, *The Meaning of Icons*;[26] Jaroslav Pelikan, *Imago Dei: The Byzantine Apologia for Icons*;[27] Michel Quenot, *The Icon: Window on the Kingdom*;[28] Daniel J. Sahas, *Icon and Logos: Sources in Eighth-Century Iconoclasm*;[29] Egon Sendler, *The Icon, Image of the Invisible: Elements of Theology, Aesthetics and Technique*;[30] St. Theodore of Studites, *St. Theodore of Studites on the Holy Icons*;[31] Bishop Kallistos Ware, *The Orthodox Way*;[32] Timothy Ware, *The Orthodox Church*;[33]

THE LITURGY ITSELF IS A FORESHADOWING OF HEAVEN

The hallmark of the Orthodox liturgy is that it transports the soul by appealing to all five senses. In doing so, it glorifies the Risen Lord and provides the worshipper with a foretaste of the joy that awaits him in Heaven. Daniel B. Clendenin, in *Eastern Orthodox Christianity*, describes the beautiful, unforgettable experience that he had, as a Protestant Christian, the first time he attended an Orthodox church in Russia:

> …the Orthodox services were…unlike anything I had ever experienced. The effect began outside the church with the glittering gold onion domes sparkling in the blue sky, and continued inside with the service itself-the chanted liturgy, bells, a cappella choirs, wafting incense, elaborate priestly vestments, and frescoes, mosaics, and icons… hundreds of burning candles in the dimly lit sanctuary… The experience was above all things aesthetic…I identified with those first emissaries of Prince Vladimir who in 988 had been awestruck at the unforgettable beauty that they had encountered in the Church of the Holy Wisdom in Constantinople…
>
> Here aesthetic beauty was employed as the means of sacred worship…Orthodox worship…is…a sacred moment, a liturgical reenactment of heaven on earth in all its beauty and transcendence, an aesthetic attempt to incarnate the present reality of the future kingdom of God.[34] It is a bold affirmation of the Incarnation of God that, as John of Damascus put in his defense of icons, "sanctifies the senses," especially the "noblest sense of sight," and permits the "glorification of matter."[35/36]

Clendenin points out that the *Philokalia*, an anthology of the early Desert Fathers, means, literally, "love of the beautiful." Orthodoxy uses beauty to captivate the senses, transport the soul, and give the worshipper a taste, a foreshadowing of the great joy that awaits him in God's Eternal Kingdom. It does this by appealing to all five senses through heavenly bells and a cappella choirs, incense mixed with myrrh, icons, royal robes of many colors, candles, kissing icons, bowing, kneeling, and tasting wine and bread.

Clendenin cites a passage from the *Russian Primary Chronicle*, in which Vladimir's emissaries describe their wonder and awe the first time they were exposed to Orthodox Christianity. Their positive experience marked the inception of the conversion of the Slavs:

> The Greeks led us to the buildings where they worship their God, and we knew not whether we were in heaven or on earth. For on earth there is no such splendor or such beauty, and we are at a loss to describe it. We know only that God dwells there among men, and their ceremonies are fairer than the ceremonies of other nations. For we cannot forget that beauty..."Orthodoxy, Sergius Bulgakov observes, "does not persuade or try to compel; it charms and attracts."[37] ...it is through its aesthetic splendor that the Orthodox liturgy witnesses to the gospel.[38]

> ...deliberate attention is given to the employment of all five of the senses...the eyes behold the icons, frescoes, and mosaics; the smell of incense symbolizes the prayers of the saints and the coming kingdom; the sense of taste is satisfied in the Eucharist; the sense of touch finds expression in the anointing of chrismation, and in kissing the Gospel, the cross, and icons; and the sense of hearing savors the chanted liturgy and a cappella choirs.[39]

The Orthodox liturgy, which glorifies the Risen Lord by involving the worshipper totally in body and mind, is often the ideal time and place for God to pour forth His mercy by performing miracles. Many miracles do occur during the liturgy and newspaper articles around the world attest to this fact. When miracles do occur in the Orthodox Church, they indicate that the barriers between Heaven and earth are, indeed, illusory; that the reality is that Heaven is ever present and at hand.

THE VENERATION OF MARY

The hallmark of Mary's personality is her willingness to submit to God's will. She is the culmination of the holy nation that God was trying to perfect in His Law and promises since Abraham: it was this nation, through its obedience to God, that would give rise to the Incarnation of God on earth, the Savior who would redeem man from his sins. Mary is worthy of the veneration of all humanity because she is ready to do the will of God. Her response to the Annunciation given by the archangel Gabriel was, "Behold the handmaid of the Lord; be it unto me according to thy word" (Luke 1:38). Both in the flesh and subsequently, in the deified state that she has attained in Heaven, Mary is and was always ready and willing to be the instrument through which God's will would be accomplished. Clendenin explains, "The Orthodox Church venerates the Virgin Mary as 'more honorable than the cherubim and beyond compare more glorious than the seraphim,' as superior to all created beings…The church of the Old Testament had for its purpose the elevation, the conservation, and the preparation of a holy humanity worthy to receive the Holy Spirit, that is, worthy of the annunciation. That holy humanity was attained in the person of the Virgin. Hence Mary is not merely the instrument, but the direct positive condition of the incarnation, its human aspect. Christ could not have been incarnate by some mechanical process that violated human nature. It was necessary for that nature itself to say for itself by the mouth of the most pure human being: 'Behold the handmaid of the Lord; be it unto me according to thy word' (Luke 1:18). At that moment the Holy Spirit descended upon her; the annunciation was the Pentecost of the Virgin, and the Spirit completely sanctified and abode with her."[40] Having attained theosis in Heaven, now she is at the right hand of her Son and continues to do God's will. She intercedes for humanity. She answers the prayers of the faithful around the world. Down through the centuries, many infirm who have asked for help have gotten miracles of healing.

The honor and respect that Orthodoxy accords to the Mother of Christ is a sign of the close spiritual relationship that the faithful have with her. The veneration of Mary, when examined within the context of God's plan for man's theosis, is the recognition that Mary has achieved God's objective for humanity, namely, union with Himself. Seen in this context, we can understand that Mary often acts not only as a conduit of God's miracles, but, because she fully retains her own identity and individuality in her deified state, she also exercises her own free will and performs miracles on her own in response to the requests of the faithful. The hierarchies of Orthodox churches of various ethnicities (Greek, Russian, Albanian, Serbian, Armenian) have authenticated miracles in which icons that depict Mary, holding the Infant Jesus, have shed tears…Mount Athos is dedicated to Mary and she often performs miracles there to assist the monks who have forsaken everything to follow Christ. An excellent examination of our ongoing, eternal friendship with Mary and the saints is provided by Sergius Bulgakov in "The Virgin and the Saints in Orthodoxy."[41]

The Orthodox Church regards Mary as the God-bearer [*Theotokos*, in Greek], Ever-Virgin [*Aeiparthenos*], All-Holy [*Panagia*], Spotless or Immaculate [*Achrantos*]. Some of these eternal characteristics have been articulated by ecumenical councils that have been held in the past. For example, she was declared to be the *Theotokos* or God-bearer by the First Ecumenical Council held at Ephesus in 431. She was declared to be the *Aeiparthenos* or Ever-Virgin by the Fifth Ecumenical Council held in Constantinople in 553. Although no council has formally declared Mary to be *Panagia* or All-Holy, the Orthodox Church has regarded her as such since the beginning. Timothy Ware, in *The Orthodox Church*, explains why Mary is regarded as All-Holy: "Among all of God's creatures, she is the supreme example of synergy or cooperation between the purpose of the deity and human freedom. God, who always respects our liberty of choice, did not wish to become incarnate without the willing consent of His Mother. He waited for her voluntary response: 'Here am I, the servant of the Lord; let it be as you have said' (Luke 1:38). Mary could have refused; she was not merely passive, but an active participant in the mystery."[42] Hence, Mary brought her will into conformity with that of God; she was cooperative and willing to be the instrument through which God's will would be accomplished on earth.

Ware points out that if Christ is the new Adam, then Mary is the new Eve. This means that Christ and Mary have fulfilled God's will through their obedience to the Father, while their predecessors, Adam and Eve, had not. Eve disobeyed God; on the contrary, Mary was obedient to God. Eve brought humanity death, the punishment for sin; Mary brought life: through her obedience, she bore Christ, who bore the penalty for our sins. Hence, since she is regarded as the new Eve, the Church hails her as *Achrantos* (Spotless) or free from actual sin. This was the condition of Adam and Eve before they disobeyed. In the hymn, *Meet It Is*, sung at the liturgy of St. John Chrysostom and other services, the Orthodox declare Mary to be the most exalted among God's creatures, "more honored than the cherubim and incomparably more glorious than the seraphim." In Orthodox liturgies and Byzantine hymns, Mary is hailed as *Theotokos, Aeiparthenos, Panagia*, and *Achrantos*.

Timothy Ware explains, "She has passed beyond death and judgment, and lives already in the Age to Come. Yet she is not thereby separated from the rest of humanity, for that same bodily glory which Mary enjoys now, all of us hope one day to share."[43] This explains why she performs miracles: she has the power to do so because she has already attained theosis or union with God.

According to Church tradition, three days after Mary's dormition (falling asleep), Christ came for her, resurrected her body, and took her to Heaven. All of the apostles, except one, Thomas, had been present for her burial. Thomas (the same doubting Thomas who put his hand in the palms and side of the Lord in the Upper Room) arrived several days later and asked to visit her tomb. However, upon his arrival, an angel of the Lord advised him that Mary's body was not there, that Christ had resurrected her, and taken her into glory in Heaven.

The Passing of Mary: Second Latin Form states that in the second year after Christ's Resurrection, His Mother, Mary, longing for her son, began to weep alone in her room. An angel of the Lord, clothed in dazzling light, appeared and greeted her. The angel presented Mary with a palm branch from the Paradise of Heaven; this palm branch glowed with exceeding white light. The angel instructed Mary to have the palm branch carried before her bier and assured her that she would be resurrected in the flesh and that she would enter into Glory on the third day.

In this account God snatched up the apostles in a cloud from the various cities in which they had been preaching the Gospel and miraculously brought them to Mary's house so that they would be present for her funeral. There was a great earthquake at Ephesus and John, who had been preaching there, was raised in a cloud before the eyes of everyone and was brought to Mary's house. When Mary died, her body glowed with a miraculous bright light. Those who were assigned to prepare her body for burial and dress her in burial clothes, could not see the form of her body because of the excessive flashing light emanating from it. A sweet scent of lily flowers emanated from her body. The apostle John carried the palm of light before her bier during the funeral procession. A circle of light appeared over her bier and an army of angels appeared in a cloud over it. Christ received her bodily into Heaven.[44]

John of Damascus, in *Three Sermons on the Dormition of the Virgin*, Sermon 2, relates that the tomb of Mary, upon inspection, was found to be empty. In this account John provides a poignant dialogue between the narrator, "I," and the empty tomb. When "I" asks the tomb where the body of the Lord's Mother is, the tomb responds that it no longer holds her, that is was powerless to hold her before divine commands:

> And you I will speak to as if living, most sacred of tombs, after the life-giving tomb of our Lord which is the source of the resurrection. Where is the pure gold which apostolic hands confided to you? Where is the inexhaustible treasure? Where the precious receptacle of God? Where is the living table? Where the new book in which the incomprehensible Word of God is written without hands? Where is the abyss of grace and the ocean of healing? Where is the life-giving fountain? Where is the sweet and loved body of God's Mother?
>
> Why do you seek in the tomb one who has been assumed to the heavenly courts? Why do you make me responsible for not keeping her? I was powerless to go against the divine commands. That sacred and holy body, leaving the winding-sheet behind, filled me full of sweet fragrance, sanctified me by its contact, and fulfilled the divine scheme, and was then assumed, angels and archangels

and all the heavenly powers escorting it. Now angels surround me, and divine grace abounds in me.[45]

We recommend the following accounts of Mary's dormition and bodily resurrection into glory: *The Departure of My Lady Mary from this World* (an English translation of six Syriac books dating to the 4th century);[46] John the Theologian, *The Book of John concerning the Falling Asleep of Mary* [*De Obitu S. Dominæ*];[47] a treatise ascribed to Joseph of Arimathea, *The Passing of Mary: First Latin Form*;[48] a treatise ascribed to Bishop Melito of Sardis, *The Passing of Mary: Second Latin Form* [*Transitus Beatæ Mariæ*];[49] Cyril of Jerusalem, *Discourse on Mary Theotokos*;[50] Evodius, *The Falling Asleep of Mary*;[51] Theodosius of Alexandria, *The Falling Asleep of Mary*;[52] John of Damascus, *Three Sermons on the Dormition of the Virgin*.[53]

Mary's bodily resurrection is a foreshadowing of Christ's return when all those asleep in Christ down through the ages will arise from their graves to meet Him in the air: "Behold, I shew you a mystery; We shall not all sleep, but we shall all be changed, In a moment, in the twinkling of an eye, at the last trump: for the trumpet shall sound, and the dead shall be raised incorruptible, and we shall be changed. For this corruptible must put on incorruption, and this mortal must put on immortality" (1 Cor 15:51-53).

On August 15 the Orthodox Church celebrates the Great Feast of the Dormition (falling asleep) of the Theotokos. On that day, the Roman Catholic Church celebrates the Assumption of Mary into Heaven. On November 1, 1950, Pope Pius XII, in *The Most Bountiful God* [*Munificentissimus Deus*], declared, "Hence the revered Mother of God...obtained, as the supreme culmination of her privileges, that she should be preserved free from the corruption of the tomb and that, like her own Son, having overcome death, she might be taken up body and soul to the glory of heaven where, as Queen, she sits in splendor at the right hand of her Son, the immortal King of the Ages… we pronounce, declare, and define it to be a divinely revealed dogma: that the Immaculate Mother of God, the ever Virgin Mary, having completed the course of her earthly life, was assumed body and soul into heavenly glory."[54] While it is the Roman Catholic Church that holds Mary's bodily Assumption into Heaven as dogma, the Orthodox Church, which has no such formal teaching, has no reason to question it.

This background material on Mary's resurrection and theosis is important in understanding the miracles that Mary has performed down through the ages in response to requests from those seeking assistance. These miracles provide empirical, reality based evidence in the physical realm that Mary has attained theosis and that she stands, in her glorified body, at the right hand of her Son in Heaven. Let us now examine some modern day miracles that have been authenticated by the hierarchy of the Orthodox Church and that have received wide media coverage.

THE WEEPING ICON OF CHICAGO

Date: December 6, 1986; September 1988; July 23, 1995
Place: St. Nicholas Albanian Orthodox Church, 2701 North
        Narragansett Avenue, Chicago, IL 60639
        (773) 889-4282
Declared to be a miraculous sign by:
        Archbishop Iakovos of the Greek Orthodox Archdiocese
        of North and South America

In front of the altar of St. Nicholas Albanian Orthodox Church there is a 3'x5' gold and scarlet canvas painting of the Virgin Mary holding the Infant Jesus. The canvas is affixed to a piece of plywood ½" in width and supported by one beam; it was installed when the church was built in 1961. The icon, part of a highly decorative wall, the iconostasis, was painted by the Manhattan artist Constantine Youssis. It was on December 6, 1986, and not coincidentally, on the Feast Day of St. Nicholas, the patron saint of the church, that the Very Reverend Archimandrite Philip Koufos first noticed moisture streaming from the hands of the Virgin. He was about to begin to celebrate the Divine Liturgy for St. Nicholas, and he was lighting the lamps in the front of the iconostasis. It was then that he first noticed moisture streaming from the hands of Mary. At first curious, then awestruck, he rushed to summon two women who had arrived early to make preparations for the liturgy, Lillian George and Bessie Tolbert, who were now in the back of the church, to come to the sanctuary to take a look. They, too, saw the moisture now gushing forth from the hand of the Virgin. Rev. Koufos fell prostrate on the floor with deep, heartfelt reverence and awe before the miraculous icon.

Soon oil was streaming from the eyes and hands of the Virgin. The oil was thin, resembling the holy oil used in the chrismation of infants, and a sweet fragrance emanated from it. Many miracles have occurred while the icon was crying and since then, more than 2 million people have visited the church to see it, at the rate of 5,000 per day, some from as far away as Pakistan and Sri Lanka.

Mitchell Locin, who covered the story for the *Chicago Tribune*, describes the occurrence thus:

> Members of a Northwest Side church were grappling Monday to understand the moisture on an icon of the Virgin Mary that made the painting appear to be weeping.

> ...a special prayer service-a paraklisis, which is a novena to the Virgin Mary-was held Monday and will be repeated daily...

When viewed Monday, the right eye of the painting glistened. Moisture streaks were visible beneath the eye and the hand of the woman Christians believe is the mother of Jesus Christ and also beneath the hand of the infant Jesus whom she holds.

…Rev. Philip Koufos, read a statement Monday afternoon:

"We interpret this phenomenon as a sign for those who may have wandered away from the church to return to Christ and his teachings for their welfare and ultimate salvation. Furthermore, we interpret this phenomenon that this could also be a sign for the suffering Orthodox Christians throughout the world for whom we should be praying…"

Father Koufos said that last Saturday, St. Nicholas Day, as he and two parishioners were lighting candles, "we discovered this moisture as we came in front of the icon of the Virgin around the eyes and dripping down. To our further amazement, we observed while we looked at the icon a spray of moisture exude from the both hands and drip down to the bottom of the icon, and since then at various times it has activated itself."

Father Koufos, who has a doctorate in archeology, said he searched for a drip from the ceiling or leaking pipes but found that "everything else appeared dry.[55]

On Sunday, December 7, 1986, 500 people jammed into the tiny church to see the icon.[56] On December 15, the *Chicago Tribune* reported that 7,000 people were visiting the church daily.[57] On December 22 and December 23, the *New York Times* and the *San Francisco Chronicle*, respectively estimated that 5,000 people a day were crowding into the church.[58] On January 14, 1987, the

Chicago Tribune advised that tens of thousands of people from all over the United States had visited the icon; the paper cited Bill Proyce, one of the church's members, who surmised that on a slow day, 2,000 to 3,000 would show up, but that on many days, it would be several thousands more than that.[59] By February 11, 1987, the *Chicago Tribune* found that 300,000 people had visited the icon to date.[60] By September 11, 1988, Rev. Philip Koufos told the *Chicago Tribune* that more than 2 million people had visited.[61]

This miraculous icon was featured on the Leeza Show and the program was rerun several times. During the interview the priest told Leeza Gibbons that he had witnessed many miracles occur before the icon. For example, when a Roman Catholic woman, holding rosary beads, entered the church and approached the icon, the rosary beads turned to gold. The priest, himself, who had suffered a leg injury while playing football in college, was miraculously healed of the disability. When Leeza asked him why it is that God chose this time and this place in which to pour forth His mercy, the priest surmised that it was because a large number of people had recently arrived from the former Soviet Union where they had not been free to practice their faith. The miracle of the weeping icon glorified God and constituted the exultant, triumphant celebration of the victory of good over evil, of Christianity over atheism, of religious freedom at long last after the extreme persecution of the Church.

The Orthodox Church had suffered great persecution under the Communist regime and priests had been executed for their faith. Between 1917 and 1935 Orthodox priests were not only arrested in Russia, many were executed by firing squads, as well. Timothy Ware, in *The Orthodox Church*, advises:

> ...in the thirty years between 1918 and 1948 more Christians died for their faith than in the three hundred years that followed Christ's Crucifixion.[62]

From October 1917, when the Bolsheviks seized power, until around 1988, the year when Russian Christianity celebrated its millennium, the Orthodox Church in the Soviet Union existed in a state of siege. The intensity of persecution varied at different points in those seventy years, but the basic attitude of the Communist authorities remained the same: religious belief, in all its manifestations, was an error to be repressed and extirpated…

The Bolsheviks, newly come to power, were quick to carry their programme into effect. Legislation in 1918 excluded the Church from all participation in the educational system, and confiscated all Church property. The Church ceased to possess any rights; quite simply, it was not a legal entity…

The bishops and clergy, in other words, could not engage in charitable or social work. Sick visiting was severely restricted; pastoral work in prisons, hospitals or psychiatric wards was impossible. Parish priests could not organize any kind of youth group or any study circle. They could not hold catechism classes or Sunday schools for children…

Not only were churches closed on a massive scale in the 1920s and 1930s, but huge numbers of bishops and clergy, monks, nuns and laity were sent to prison and to concentration camps. How many were executed or died from ill-treatment we simply cannot calculate. Nikita Struve provides a list of martyr-bishops running to 130 names, and even this he terms "provisional and incomplete." The sum total of priest-martyrs must extend to tens of thousands…Nothing on a remotely comparable scale had happened in the persecutions under the Roman Empire.[63]

An example of the persecution to which Orthodox Christians were submitted under Communist rule is seen in the life of St. Tikhon, the Patriarch of Moscow. During the years 1917-1925, St. Tikhon took a vociferous stand against the atheist Bolsheviks and he anathematized them. From May 1922 to June 1923 he was imprisoned for his faith and his outspokenness; when released from prison in 1923, he was forced to soften his words in documents that he wrote about the Church's stance against the atheist regime; in 1925 he died under mysterious circumstances. Undoubtedly, St. Tikhon was a martyr. The unexplained situation regarding his treatment in prison, his forced statements under torture, and untimely death is not only tragic, but chilling.[64]

Ware advises that before St. Tikhon died, he appointed three clerics to be the guardians of the Patriarchate. Two of them, Metropolitans Cyril and Agathangel, were in prison when St. Tikhon died, and hence, could not succeed him. The third, Metropolitan Peter, was arrested, exiled to Siberia, and he remained there until his death in 1936.[65] During the years 1959-1964 Khrushchev renewed the persecution of the Church; in 1964-1988 a dissident movement emerged, but was crushed.[66]

Excellent books addressing the persecution of the Church under Communist rule are as follows: Walter Kolarz, *Religion in the Soviet Union*;[67] Dimitry Pospielovsky, *The Russian Church under the Soviet Regime 1917-1982*;[68] Nikita A. Struve, *Christians in Contemporary Russia*;[69] Timothy Ware, *The Orthodox Church*.[70]

Albania, like Russia, also experienced government efforts to eradicate Christianity through persecution. Ware advises:

> Conditions were worst of all for the Church of Albania, which had been granted autocephaly in 1937 by the Patriarchate of Constantinople. In 1967 the government of Hoxha announced that Albania was now

the first truly atheist state in the world: every place of worship had been closed and every visible expression of religious faith eliminated. Repression fell with equal severity on Orthodox, Roman Catholics and Muslims. The last primate of the Albanian Orthodox church, Archbishop Damian, died in prison in 1973. In 1991, when religion began to emerge from underground, no Orthodox bishops at all had survived, and less than twenty Orthodox priests were still alive, half of them too infirm to officiate. Churches are now being reopened, new clergy ordained, and a small theological school has been started. In 1992 Bishop Anastasios (Yannoulatos), a Greek who has worked as a missionary in East Africa, was appointed head of the Albanian Church; he has declared his willingness to resign as soon as a suitable Albanian candidate can be found.[71]

Hence, 1986 marked the first time that many emigrés from the former Soviet Union had ever set foot in a church or attended a liturgy. The clergy of St. Nicholas Albanian Orthodox Church understood that the miracle of the weeping holy icon in their midst was a celebration of the glorification of God, the victory of religious freedom, and the triumph of the Bride of Christ over the forces of evil. The priest relating the miracle to Leeza Gibbons on her television program reminded the audience that Christ had proclaimed, "…upon this rock I will build my church; and the gates of hell shall not prevail against it" (Mat 16:18). Miracles often happen concurrently with political events as a sign of celebration, to proclaim the glory of God, or to provide hope in the face of adversity and persecution.

Daniel B. Clendenin, in *Eastern Orthodox Christianity*, reminds us that Christ foretold the persecution of His Church so that we would expect it when it happened:

Jesus warned his followers about persecution on his account (Mat 5:10-11; 10:18; 22; 13:21; 24:9). Luke records the fulfillment of that warning (Acts 5:41). Every epistle of Paul except Titus mentions Christian suffering, either of Paul or of his readers. The books of Hebrews, James, especially Peter, Jude, and Revelation all witness to the reality of suffering in the life of the early church… Paul taught that God is to be discovered not so much through his startling displays of power and miraculous interventions, but through times of great suffering, testing, and human weakness (2 Cor 12:7-10). Orthodox believers have experienced this sobering truth. May we in the West have the grace and wisdom to learn from their experience, rejecting our triumphalistic attitudes in favor of the more biblical idea of knowing God through the way of the cross.[72]

Historically, whenever the Church was persecuted, miracles have occurred, such as the renewing of icons. Lossky, in *The Mystical Theology of the Eastern Church*, declares, "In every place where the faith has been put to the test, there have been abundant outpourings of grace, the most astonishing miracles-icons renewing themselves before the eyes of astonished spectators; the cupolas of churches shining with a light not of this world."[73] Ware cites Lossky and in a footnote appends this fact: "The miraculous 'renewal of icons,' to which Lossky refers, has occurred in a number of places under Communist rule. Icons and frescoes, darkened and disfigured with age, have suddenly and without any human intervention resumed fresh and light colours."[74]

It is facts such as these, and a study of the executions committed en masse of Orthodox clergy under Communist rule, that makes it evident why the priest of St. Nicholas Albanian Orthodox Church understood that the miracle of the weeping icon was given by God as a declaration of victory over the forces of evil and to strengthen the faith of new Christians who were attending church for the first time in their lives.

While the icon commenced weeping in December 1986, it eventually stopped and then began again on two other occasions. In September 1988 moisture reappeared on the Face of the Virgin and remained there for two weeks. On July 23, 1995 the miraculous icon recommenced weeping, this time, as profusely and prolifically as it had originally done on December 6, 1986.

In addition, myrrh, the fragrant herb, is reported to have started flowing from the right hand of the Virgin. Myrrh is an aromatic gum resin used as an ingredient in perfume and incense. Myrrh was one of the gifts that the Three Magi brought from the East to Bethlehem to celebrate the birth of the infant Jesus (Mat 2:11). Because of its strong, heavenly, other worldly fragrance, it is burned in censers in churches to honor God. It is significant that myrrh emanated from the hand of the Virgin as she is depicted holding the Infant Jesus: historically, myrrh has been known to possess curative properties and to promote healing. In the past myrrh has been used as an astringent and today the tincture of myrrh continues to be used in pharmacology: it permits shrinkage of mucous membranes and exposed tissue, is used internally to stop hemorrhaging, and provides relief from cuts, insect bites, and fungal infections. Therefore, myrrh connotes recovered health and healing from past wounds. The pouring forth of myrrh from the hand of the Virgin is emblematic of the spiritual healing that Christ provides, of His redemption of man from his fallen state after Adam's disobedience, and of the everlasting union of man with God (theosis) that awaits followers of Christ. It proclaims the Good News to all the world: that Christ was born to heal the rupture between man and God. Furthermore, the scent of myrrh is delightful, it fills the senses, and lifts the heart, reminding us of the joy that awaits us in God's Kingdom and of Christ's first words to the women bearing spices after His

Resurrection on Sunday morning: "Rejoice!" (Mat 28:9). Thus, its sweet appeal to the senses that elevates our mood provides an iconic representation in the physical realm of the spiritual joy that awaits us in Christ's Kingdom.

Although the weeping from this particular icon eventually ceased, the miracles did not: tears taken from it were used to anoint other icons and these icons began to cry as well.

There has been prolific media coverage of this miraculous holy icon: newspapers that covered the story include the *Chicago Tribune*, the *Houston Chronicle*, the *Los Angeles Times*, the *New York Times*, and the *San Francisco Chronicle* . The miracle was often featured as front pages news. We recommend the following newspaper articles: Mitchell Locin, "Weeping Icon Draws Worshipers," *Chicago Tribune*, December 9, 1986, 3; Mitchell Locin, "Icon's Tears Bring Smiles to Parishioners," *Chicago Tribune*, December 12, 1986, 1; "Weeping Icon Watched," *Houston Chronicle*, December 12, 1986, 10; Tasia Kavvadias, "Icon's Miraculous Sign Draws Multitude," *Chicago Tribune*, December 15, 1986, 1; "Weeping Virgin Icon Draws Throngs to Chicago," *New York Times*, December 22, 1986, B16; "Throngs Flock to Weeping Virgin," *San Francisco Chronicle*, December 23, 1986, 12; Wes Smith, "Icon, Air Controller Get Credit in Miracle," *Chicago Tribune*, December 31, 1986, 1; "Weeping Icon Called Miraculous Sign," *Los Angeles Times*, January 3, 1987, 13; Michael Locin, "Visitors to Icon Force Church to Cut its Hours," *Chicago Tribune*, January 14, 1987, 8; Elaine Sarlas, "Weeping Icon," *Chicago Tribune*, January 27, 1987, 10; Bruce Buursma, "Greek Orthodox Leader Calls Weeping Madonna Icon a Sign, Not a Miracle," *Chicago Tribune*, February 11, 1987, 3; "Weeping Icon Stops its Crying," *Chicago Tribune*, July 18, 1987, 5; Jessica Seigel, "Faithful Gather to See Icon's Tears," *Chicago Tribune*,

September 11, 1988, 3; and Paul Galloway, "And Now, the Tears Flow Again; Church Takes Low-key Tack with Icon's Latest Weeping," *Chicago Tribune*, July 26, 1995, 1.

BLOOD GUSHES FORTH FROM COMMUNION BREAD

<u>Date:</u>   April 21, 1991
<u>Place:</u>   Zarka, Jordan
<u>Authenticated by:</u>
      Diodorus I, Patriarch of Jerusalem

As a priest was preparing Communion bread in a church in the working class community of Zarka, near Amman, blood spurted forth from the Communion bread and filled a brass holder. When the priest cried out, startled, and with awe, the parishioners rushed forward to take some of the blood. The miracle was reported in the *Houston Chronicle*, which relates the event thus:

> ...Communion bread began spouting blood at a Jordanian church last week.

> ...blood appeared to pour from the bread, spilling into a brass holder.

> The priest's screams prompted a rush of worshipers to the altar. "They started daubing it on their faces and eating it," said the mother superior of a local convent school.

> "You couldn't control them any more," Bishop Constinos of Jordan said, gazing at the brass plate holding a small silver box containing two cubes of moist-looking, bright red bread-all that was left.[75]

Church officials also relate that another miracle had also occurred concurrently at the home of an elderly parishioner who was dying. The moment that the blood spurted forth from the bread in the church, an elderly man who lay dying in his bed at home ripped off his oxygen mask, jumped out of bed, got dressed, and went to church, telling his wife that something had happened at the church.

The Patriarch of Jerusalem, Diodorus I, journeyed to Jordan to investigate the miracle. He concluded that it was, indeed, a miracle, and took the two squares of bread, covered in blood, back to Jerusalem for veneration. He returned them to Jordan where a shrine was made for them.

We find it significant that the miracle occurred after the Gulf War ended. The Gulf War had lasted from January 17, 1991 until February 28, 1991. God's mercy poured forth in the Middle East as a sign of His infinite love, which may be contrasted to the unspeakable atrocities that America's relentless imperialism precipitated that year. Looking backward, we now understand that it was a road sign on the highway of time that reminds us that Orthodox Christians were living peacefully and were permitted to practice their religion in a Muslim country. The proliferation of Orthodox miracles at that time constituted undeniable landmarks indicating that everything would change, that a phony religious war between Christianity and Islam, created to facilitate western adventurism and imperialism, was morphing into shape.

It was also a sign to Muslims, who also came and saw, that the Orthodox Church is the true Church of Jesus Christ on earth, that His mercy is infinite, and that the atrocities of American imperialism must not be confused with true Christianity.

It must also be pointed out that in 1991 Jordan and Syria were accepting Iraqi exiles who were fleeing the chaos that had erupted in their own country after the Gulf War. God's mercy miraculously poured forth in Jordan at a time when Iraqi refugees were steadily streaming into that country for shelter. The miracle was a sign that God was watching and that Heaven is near to displaced Iraqi Orthodox refugees living in Jordan.

THE MIRACULOUS ICON OF OUR LADY OF CICERO

<u>Date:</u>   April 22, 1994
<u>Place:</u> St. George Antiochian Orthodox Church, 1220 South
        60ᵗʰ Court, Cicero, IL 60804, (708) 656-2927
<u>Authenticated by:</u>
        the Antiochian Archdiocese in 1994-first by Bishop Basil
        and immediately following by Metropolitan Philip,
        Metropolitan of All North America

On Friday evening, April 22, 1994, as priests were preparing for an evening worship service, a visiting priest from All Saints Orthodox Church in Chicago first noticed that water was flowing from the eyes of the Virgin Mary in a gold and blue icon of Mary holding the Infant Jesus in the church sanctuary. He immediately asked the other priests whether anyone had anointed the icon with holy water. When it was learned that no one had, they understood that they were witnessing a miracle.

When the icon began to cry, the church immediately notified the American hierarchy of the Antiochian Orthodox Church. Bishop Basil was in Pittsburg at the time when he was instructed to go to Cicero as soon as possible to investigate the phenomenon. On April 25 Bishop Basil arrived at the church and asked to see the icon. First he carefully scrutinized both sides and then did something that every Orthodox priest must do in this situation: he conducted a very brief exorcism in order to ascertain whether the manifestation was divine in origin or demonic. Michael Hirsley, who covered the story in a front page article in the *Chicago Tribune*, writes, "Even as he saw the 'weeping' icon, inspected it front and back, and was moved by what he saw, Basil said his instructions and instinct were to 'test the spirit.' 'Everything that appears miraculous is not from God,' he said."[76]

Indeed this is true. Let us digress very briefly and examine why necessity dictated that Bishop Basil conduct an exorcism of the icon. There is textual evidence in both the Old and New Testaments that the principalities of darkness have a limited ability to perform miracles. While the OT affirms that miracles do, indeed, exist, it distinguishes between miracles and magic (sorcery) and gives examples of both.

For example, Moses casts his rod on the ground and it becomes a serpent (Ex 4:3).[6] Then he puts forth his hand, catches the serpent by the tail and it becomes a rod again (Ex 4:4). He puts his hand in his bosom, withdraws it and it is as leprous as snow (Ex 4:6). He puts his hand back into his bosom, withdraws it again, and it is healed (Ex 4:7). Moses and Aaron go before Pharaoh: Aaron casts down his rod and it becomes a serpent (Ex 7:10). However, the reader is surprised to learn that Pharaoh's sorcerers can do the same thing: "they also did in like manner with their enchantments" (Ex 7:11). Here we see that while servants of the one true God can perform miracles, sorcerers can perform magic by the power of the prince of darkness.

However, then there is still yet another surprise: Aaron's rod swallows up the rods of Pharaoh's sorcerers: "For they cast down every man his rod, and they became serpents: but Aaron's rod swallowed up their rods" (Ex 7:12). Here we see a sharp distinction between the infinite power of the Living God and the finite

---

6   Copyright © 2008 from *An Eastern Orthodox View of Pascal* by Mary Efrosini Gregory. Reprinted by permission of Light & Life Publishing Company.

abilities of the prince of darkness. God is the Creator; the prince of darkness is merely a created being. God is limitless; the latter is limited. The OT offers this event as an iconic representation of the existence of an evil created being that has been given limited power on the earth. Hence, in Ex 7:8-12, the Bible distinguishes between miracles and magic (sorcery).

Then the OT narrates the ten plagues that God sends to Egypt. It is significant that Pharaoh's sorcerers can duplicate the first two plagues, but not the remaining eight: their powers are limited. In the first plague, Aaron lifts up his rod and the water in the Nile River turns into blood (Ex 7:20). The fish die, the river stinks, the water becomes undrinkable; there is blood in all the vessels in Egypt as well, in both the wooden ones and in those made of stone (Ex 7:21). Pharaoh's sorcerers were able to duplicate this first plague: "And the magicians of Egypt did so with their enchantments" (Ex 7:22).

In the second plague, Aaron stretches his hand over the waters of Egypt and frogs come forth and cover the land of Egypt (Ex 8:6). Pharaoh's sorcerers are able to duplicate this feat: "And the magicians did so with their enchantments, and brought up frogs upon the land of Egypt" (Ex 8:7).

However, Aaron and Moses perform eight more miracles (plagues upon Egypt), but Pharaoh's sorcerers are unable to duplicate them. This shows that the powers and principalities of darkness are limited, as they are created beings. In the third plague, Aaron stretches out his hand with his rod and turns the dust of the earth into lice (the KJV says "lice"; the NIV, "gnats"). This lice infects man and beast throughout all of Egypt (Ex 8:17). However, Pharaoh's sorcerers cannot duplicate this feat: "And the magicians did so with their enchantments to bring forth lice, but they could not" (Ex 8:18). The fourth plague was flies (Ex 8:20-32); the fifth plague was against livestock (Ex 9:1-7); the sixth plague was boils (Ex 9:8-12); the seventh plague was hail (Ex 9:13-35); the eighth plague was locusts (Ex 10:1-20); the ninth plague was darkness (Ex 10:21-29); the tenth plague was the death of the firstborn (Ex 11:1-10).

The OT also provides us with a glimpse of the prince of darkness having a conversation with God (Job 1:6-12; 2:1-7). Here he is the accuser: God permits him entry into Heaven and he accuses Job. Many ask why God would allow this. St. Peter of Damaskos has the answer: Peter teaches us that God allows the elect to be tempted according to the strength of each so that the fallen angels may be mocked and, with God's help, defeated by the elect.[77]

We see him again in the NT when he tempts Christ in the wilderness and then sets Him upon the pinnacle of the Temple (Mat 4:1-11; Mark 1:12-13; Luke 4:1-13). He tempts Christ because he rejects the reality that he is merely a created being and, desiring to be someone that he is not, namely, the Creator, Himself, he wants to be worshipped. We understand that he wants to be someone that he is not and that he is futilely attempting to grasp a lie. He spends his time trying to convince others of lies and feels a sense of power when he succeeds in deceiving them. When Christ conducts exorcisms of demoniacs (ie: the demoniac of the Gadarenes in Mark 5:1-20; Luke 8:26-39), we get another glimpse of how the realm of the lie can destroy lives.

The spiritual realm is real and the Orthodox Church, guided by Scriptural teaching, acknowledges the necessity of conducting exorcisms. The Orthodox Church exorcizes the icon as a precautionary measure and, if the icon continues to weep, it is considered not to be a demonic manifestation. After the exorcism the faithful are free to venerate Mary through the object.

The Very Rev. Nicholas Dahdal, pastor of St. George Antiochian Orthodox Church, explained to the *Chicago Tribune* why he believed that Mary has performed this miracle:

> "It is said that the Mother of God weeps for her lost children, as a loving mother would," Dahdal said. "She weeps because of the hatred, suffering and immorality that has plagued our world and our hearts. She calls upon each one to change in this world by remembering and acting upon the teachings and life of her son, our Savior Jesus Christ."[78]

The Most Reverend Metropolitan Philip (Saliba), Archbishop of the Antiochian Orthodox Church of the Diocese New York and Washington, DC, and Metropolitan of the Antiochian Orthodox Church of all North America, declared the miracle to be authentic.

By May 15, 1994, the icon was still weeping. Eric Zorn of the *Chicago Tribune*, in a front page story, reported that liquid continued to flow from the eyes of the Virgin and that by then thousands of visitors had seen the icon.[79] In his coverage Mr. Zorn took a very fair and open minded stance and examined circumstances surrounding the miracle that attest to its authenticity. He pointed out that St. George Antiochian Orthodox Church is not asking for any money or retribution:

The Antiochian Orthodox Church has roots back to the time of Christ and has operated in this country since 1895. No amusement parks, road shows or 800 numbers. The church in Cicero does not even pass a collection plate or set out a donation box, not even now that attendance at mass has increased at least fivefold since the icon's tears were first reported April 22.[80]

At this juncture one should add that the Antiochian Orthodox Church traces its roots directly back to the first century Antioch, the city in which the disciples of Jesus Christ were first called Christians (Acts 11:26). The Antiochian Orthodox Christian Archdiocese of North America explains its history, beliefs, organizational hierarchy and provides an online liturgical guide at its webside, http://www.antiochian.org/about.

By July 15 the icon was still crying, public interest in the miraculous icon continued to be strong and visitors were swamping the church. Rev. Nicholas Dahdal informed the *Chicago Tribune* that it was necessary to keep the doors to the church open from 11 am to 8 pm because of the huge volume of visitors.[81] Pilgrims from as far away as Finland, the Philippines, and the Middle East came to see the icon.

When visitors came to St. George, they requested anointment of the tears. In order to fulfill their requests, the priests mixed the tears from the holy icon with olive oil and then dipped cotton swabs into the mixture. Rev. Dahdal informed the *Chicago Tribune* that more than 100,000 cotton swabs dipped in the mixture of tears and oil had been distributed to the visiting public.[82] In addition, he distributed small containers of the mixture to more than 1,000 churches so that the priests in those churches could anoint their own parishioners.[83]

The Miracle at St. George's has received ample coverage by the press, often on the front page. We recommend the following articles: Penny Roberts, "Many Find Miracle in Weeping Mary," *Chicago Tribune*, April 25, 1994, 3; Michael Hirsley, "Icon's Tears are Turning into a Stream of People," *Chicago Tribune*, May 6, 1994, 1; Eric Zorn, "Icon Is Still Crying for our Attention," *Chicago Tribune* May 15, 1994, 1; Henri E. Cauvin, "Believers Still Flock to Cicero Icon," *Chicago Tribune*, July 15, 1994, 8.

THE BLINKING AND WEEPING ICON OF CHRIST

Date: Week of Oct. 27, 1996
Place: Church of the Nativity, Bethlehem, West Bank
Authenticated by:
Father Anastasios on behalf of the Greek Orthodox
Patriarchate of Jerusalem

On Nov. 28, 1996 Associated Press Television (APTV) did a story on a continuing miracle that was occurring in the Church of the Nativity in Manger Square, Bethlehem.

The Church of the Nativity is the site of Christ's birthplace. In 326 when St. Helena visited the Holy Land, she began construction of this church. Today the precise spot where the Lord was born 2,000 years ago is encased in white marble: in the midst of this piece of marble there is situated a magnificent silver star with 14 points; fifteen lamps burn along the periphery of the star. Photographs of this spectacular silver star are posted on the Internet in travel guides such as www.atlastours.net and www.sacred-destinations.com.[84]

Facing the site of the Lord's birthplace is a column on which a fourth century icon of Christ has been painted. On Nov. 28, 1996 APTV reported that four weeks prior (the week of October 27), a group of tourists who were visiting the church had witnessed a sudden flash of light that burst forth from the icon. This initial phenomenon was followed by the icon's blinking and weeping. In its program APTV cited George Hintilian, an Armenian Orthodox Christian, Jerusalem historian, and author of eight books on Christianity, who described the beginning days of the miracle. We take our dialogue directly from the transcript available on APTV's online archives:

George Hintlian, an Armenian Christian who is an expert on Christianity, says the miracle has been seen by reliable witnesses.

SOUNDBITE: (English)

"According to reliable sources at the Greek patriarchates and according to witnesses with whom I talked, at that moment there was a group of tourists and there was a shaft of light which came and Jesus' eyes were closing and opening-it was just a minute-and some say that there were tears coming down the cheeks. I mean this is not anything unusual because it has happened before the great earthquake in 1927 when similar things happened within the Church of Nativity. But this is according to some locals and to myself a kind of affirmation of the presence of Christ according to the Greek patriarchates, they say that this is a sign of coming times."[85]

Greek Orthodox Palestinians, who trace their roots directly back to Christ, surmised that the miracle might be a sign of troubled times ahead. APTV reported:

60-year-old Madlein Zoghbi is one of thousands of Christians who have visited to the centuries-old icon in the past few weeks.

Zoghbi says the crying Jesus isn't a good sign.

SOUNDBITE: (Arabic)

"It means sad days. When Jesus cries and his tears flow, that means he is sad for us because we might have a disaster. May God protect us."

SUPER CAPTION: Madlein Zoghbi, Palestinian Christian[86]
In addition, resident Islamic Palestinians witnessed the miracle and were struck by it:

> Sadika Hamida, a Muslim woman who has been working in the church as a cleaner for the past 20 years, was also present.

SOUNDBITE: (Arabic)

> "As I looked, I saw the icon blinking. I watched carefully as it blinked and made my wish to open the hearts of people to love each other and respect the church."

SUPER CAPTION: Sadika Hamida. Muslim cleaner at the Church. CNN's website posts a photograph of Ms. Hamida and cites her statement:

> "They were real tears, red tears," Hamida said. "It was beautiful, so beautiful."[87]

CNN also reported that Father Anastasios, the Bethlehem representative of the Greek Orthodox Patriarchate of Jerusalem, authenticated the miracle, as he had witnessed it himself: "I saw him closing and opening his eyes."[88]

The *Jerusalem Post*, in two articles, confirmed that the Patriarchate had authenticated the miracle:

> Church leaders here are calling a modern miracle a painting of Jesus on a marble column in the Basilica of the Nativity, which they say has begun "weeping."

> "I have seen it myself," said Father Anastasios, the official representative in Bethlehem of Jerusalem's Greek Orthodox Archbishop Diodoros.

Nonclerical witnesses also have claimed that they actually have seen tears emerge from the painting, which is located above the Grotto of the Nativity, believed by many to be the exact spot where Jesus was born...

"Many people have seen the tears," said Father Anastasios. "It is officially declared a great miracle."

"Jesus is crying because the world is not going well."[89]

On November 29, 1996 Karin Laub, an Associated Press writer, reported in the *Times- Picayune* that the icon of Christ began to blink. She pointed out that Father Anastasios authenticated the miracle on behalf of the Greek Orthodox Patriarchate of Jerusalem and declared that he had seen the icon weep himself. Here are some of the comments that were reported in the press beginning with the *Times-Picayune*:

Her hands clasped in prayer, a Palestinian seamstress stared intently at an icon of Jesus painted on a column in the Church of the Nativity, just above the grotto where tradition says Jesus was born.

"Look, look," she said. Jesus' face was barely visible in the shadows of the candle-lighted basilica. "He blinked. What a blessing."

Nadia Banoura is one of thousands of Christians to visit the centuries-old icon since Greek Orthodox priests said they saw Jesus blink six weeks ago and declared it a miracle.

"It's a message for people to come back to God and religion," said Father Anastasios, the senior Greek Orthodox clergyman in Bethlehem.

...a steady stream of Palestinian Christians, and even some Muslims, filed past the icon this week. Some said they could see Jesus blink...[90]

The prolific press coverage of the miracle frequently cited Christians who voiced their belief that the crying Jesus was announcing troubled times ahead. Believers surmised that God was foretelling future political turmoil. History has proven them to be correct and it has also revealed why God chose this time and place to weep tears of blood.

APTV reported that the miracle commenced during the week of October 27, 1996. On December 22, 1995 Israel had returned control of the West Bank to Yasser Arafat and the Palestinian Authority. Therefore, the 1996 miracle ushered in Bethlehem's second year under Palestinian rule.

On December 24, 1995, the *Times-Picayune* reported that Arafat had declared, "We pronounce this holy land, this holy city, the city of the Palestinian Jesus, a liberated city forever, forever, forever!... Tomorrow my brother Elias and I will celebrate together and for the first time the birth of our Lord Jesus Christ under the Palestinian flag...And tomorrow we shall meet and pray in Jerusalem at the Al Aqsa Mosque and the Church of the Holy Sepulcher."[91]

However, Arafat was to demonstrate contempt for Christianity. The Islamic religion takes an adversarial position to Christ: it denies His Death and Resurrection, and His Deity. In fact, throughout the Dome of the Rock there are engraved messages that deny that God could have ever had a Son.

Furthermore, Arafat's wife, Suha, desecrated the silver star that marks the precise location of the Lord's birth when she chose to place her own baby atop it and display mock piety. On December 24, 1995, in a front page story, the *New York Times* reported:

Mr. Arafat's wife preceded him to Bethlehem by a day with their five-month-old daughter, Zahwa. Before Mr. Arafat arrived today, Mrs. Arafat, who converted from Christianity to Islam on marrying the Palestinian leader, entered the Church of the Nativity and descended with her child into the crypt revered as the site of Jesus' birth. There, crossing herself and getting on her knees, she placed Zahwa on the star marking the traditional place where Jesus lay, and stayed a while in prayer.[92]

This is the ultimate affront to the Lord and an iconic representation of how the forces of darkness mimic piety and offer a cheap facsimile of faith in a lame attempt to strike against God. History has shown that Ms. Arafat's sacrilege was merely an entrée to violence culminating in death: gun battles and hostage taking would besiege the Church of the Nativity in the future.

Contrary to Arafat's initial demonstrations of peace, the Palestinian Authority not only did not cease its terrorist activities, it increased them and violence gradually reached a crescendo. By March 10, 2002, Serge Schmemann, in the *New York Times*, summarized the state of affairs that existed in the land of Christ's birth at that time:

Everything is different from what it was, or should have been. Only in the last week, an Israeli motorcyclist was shot dead in the Judean desert, a suicide bomber was disarmed in the best-known café of Jerusalem's trendy German Colony, and one of the most popular Tel Aviv nightspots was savaged by a Palestinian wielding an M-16, grenades and a knife. Jericho is off limits. Parents try to keep children out of malls, crowded cafés, buses. Reservists say goodbye differently now when they leave for active duty.

...Going from Bethlehem to a nearby village now takes a Palestinian four hours, when it's possible at all. The bombs spread terror at night, the gunfire in the day. The Church of the Nativity in Bethlehem, a mainstay of pilgrims for centuries and the livelihood for generations here, is empty save for three Armenian monks and two people praying in the spot where tradition says Jesus was born.

The souvenir shops on the square outside are shuttered up...walls...are papered over with portraits of "martyrs"- local youths killed in the 17-month uprising...

The Holy Land has become a war zone with no front. It is not only the terror and the fear, but the conversations, the headlines, the confessions of despair and the grasping for slivers of hope...[93]

Tragically, Palestinian terrorism in Bethlehem reached a peak when Arabs lay siege to the Church of the Nativity and occupied it at gunpoint the following month. On April 2, 2002, armed Palestinian terrorists invaded the site of the Lord's birthplace and occupied it in the midst of 200 nuns and priests. They were fleeing Israel's Operation Defensive Shield which was responding to suicide bombings in West Bank locations. For 38 consecutive days, from April 2-May 10, 2002, the world watched on television as gunmen occupied the church. The Palestinian Arabs who took residence inside the church desecrated it beyond belief: they urinated everywhere; used toilet paper was strewn about; the militants ripped up Bibles and used the pages as toilet paper.

Eventually some of the trapped Christians inside the church were released. One by one, 95 hostages were set free. Finally, 38 days after its onset, the crisis ended through negotiations.

However, after the occupiers had left the premises, the Israel Defense Forces (IDF) found 40 explosive devices inside the church.

The Prince of Peace has come to earth bringing divine gifts-eternal life and the union of God and man (theosis). However, He was rejected by His own, just as the Bible had predicted, and by Mohammedans. Indeed, the tears of blood that commenced flowing from His holy icon during the week of October 27, 1996, did announce impending tragic events both at that site and throughout Israel, as well. It reminds us that 2,000 years ago Christ wept over Jerusalem as He looked into the future and saw the unspeakable tragedy that would occur when Titus would lay siege to Jerusalem and the Temple in 70 AD (Luke 19:41-44). Tinnelus Rufus, under the aegis of Hadrian, would plow the area of the Temple in 135 AD.

At this juncture let us briefly examine why the Koran is a fake gospel and how it sets itself in opposition to the Bible.[94] An understanding of the contempt that the Koran articulates for God the Father, the Son, and the Holy Spirit will make it readily evident as to why Ms. Arafat felt compelled to mock the silver star that marks the birthplace of Christ and why the Palestinian militants desecrated the Church of the Nativity during the 38 days that they occupied it.

First, the God of the Christians and the Jews is clearly not the Allah of the Muslims: the God of the Bible can do only good, while Allah of the Koran performs both good and evil deeds. The Bible specifies, "And God saw everything that he had made, and, behold, it was very good" (Gen 1:31); "Let no man say when he is tempted, I am tempted of God: for God cannot be tempted with evil, neither tempteth he any man" (Jas 1:13).

However, the Allah of Islam is the creator of both good and evil. The Koran continually reiterates that Allah does evil: "Say, I seek refuge in the Lord of the daybreak, from the evil of what He has created" (Surah 113:1-2).[95] Here Allah creates evil. Furthermore, Allah chooses to withhold guidance from men and he also leads them astray: "And if We had so willed, We could have given every soul its guidance, but..." (Surah 32:13).[96] Here Allah is bragging that he could have lead men along the path of righteousness, but he has deliberately chosen not to; the implication is that he deliberately lets people go astray rather than even bothering to enlighten them. This is a familiar theme in the Koran: "Then Allah sendeth whom He will astray, and guideth whom He will" (Surah 14:4).[97] Here we go a step further: Allah not only withholds guidance, he actually forces people to err! In the Koran Allah deceives humanity on several occasions and guides it along the path of error: "What aileth you that ye are become two parties regarding the hypocrites, when Allah cast them back (to disbelief) because of what they earned? Seek ye to guide him whom Allah hath sent astray? He whom Allah sendeth astray, for him thou (O Muhammad) canst not find a road" (Surah 4:88).[98] In this single verse the Koran articulates three times that Allah forces people to err and that they have no free will in the matter: "Allah cast them back (to disbelief); "Allah hath sent astray"; "whom Allah sendeth astray." Elsewhere, Allah sets a seal on men's hearts so that it is impossible for them ever to believe: "As to those who reject Faith, It is the same to them Whether thou warn them Or do not warn them; they will not believe. God hath set a seal On their hearts and on their hearing, And on their eyes is a veil" (Surah 2:6-7).[99] Allah could have saved everyone and given everyone the true faith, but he chose not to and decided to deliberately lead men astray: "Had Allah willed He could have made you (all) one nation, but He sendeth whom He will astray and guideth whom He will, and ye will indeed be asked of what ye used to do" (Surah 16:93).[100] Here Allah doesn't get mad, he gets even. Allah is moody, subject to the fluctuating levels of serotonin in his brain, vicious, and vindictive. He is also somewhat of a reformed theologian, embracing double predestination and the election of the damned: he chooses whom he will save and whom he will damn. The Koran goes on, "They schemed-but God also schemed. God is most profound in His machinations" (Surah 8:30).[101] Because the Koran continually reiterates that Allah does both good and evil and portrays him as deceiving people on many occasions and guiding them along the path of error, one must necessarily extrapolate that Muslims worship the prince of darkness. Furthermore, Allah, who is the author of evil, does not grieve over sins. In fact, behavior that is considered sinful on earth is allowed in heaven: extramarital sex and polygamy are given as reward (Surah 2:25; 4:57; 56:35-38).

Having seen that the Koran blasphemes God the Father by negating the goodness of His nature, let us now examine the contempt that it demonstrates for the Holy Trinity. The Koran continually and obsessively reiterates hatred for God the Son: "O ye people of the Book! overstep not bounds in your religion; and of God, speak only truth. The Messiah, Jesus, son of Mary, is only an apostle of God, and his Word which he conveyed into Mary, and a Spirit proceeding from himself. Believe therefore in God and his apostles, and say not, 'Three:' (there is a Trinity)-Forbear-it will be better for you. God is only one God! Far be it from His glory that He should have a son! His, whatever is in the Heavens, and whatever is in the Earth! And God is a sufficient Guardian" (Surah 4:171).[102] This incoherent stream is merely a perversion of the Bible. Basically, it is taking the position that Jesus (Isa, in some translations), the son of Mary (Marium), is merely an apostle of Allah; it specifically forbids Muslims from recognizing that God is Three Persons in One; it arrogantly declares, "Far be it from His glory that He should have a son!" The Koran clearly denies the preexistence of Christ. Let us see the difference between the Bible and the Koran on this point: the apostle John says of Christ, "All things were made by him;

and without him was not any thing made that was made" (John 1:3). Christ is the Creator of the universe and everything in it; therefore, He preexists. However, the Koran rejects the preexistence of Jesus: "the likeness of Jesus with Allah is as the likeness of Adam. He created him of dust, then He said unto him: Be! and he is" (Surah 3:59).[103] Thus, the Koran distorts the Bible and claims, rather, that the Father created Christ from the dust of the earth as he did Adam; that the dust of the earth antecedes Christ; that the universe was here before Christ; that Christ was merely a mortal, as was Adam.

The vendetta against Christ is endless and obsessive: God would never have a son, far be it from him, the heavens and earth would split open and the mountains would fall if he did, and the diatribes go on and on: "And they say: The Beneficent hath taken unto Himself a son. Assuredly ye utter a disastrous thing Whereby almost the heavens are torn, and the earth is split asunder and the mountains fall in ruins, That ye ascribe unto the Beneficent a son, When it is not meet for (the Majesty of) the Beneficent that he should choose a son" (Surah 19:88-92);[104] "It befitteth not (the Majesty of) Allah that He should take unto Himself a son" (Surah 19:35).[105]

The Koran also denies the Crucifixion and Resurrection of Christ. First, it articulates that Christ was never crucified: "And because of their saying: We slew the Messiah, Jesus son of Mary, Allah's messenger-they slew him not nor crucified him, but it appeared so unto them; and lo! those who disagree concerning it are in doubt thereof; they have no knowledge thereof save pursuit of a conjecture; they slew him not for certain" (Surah 4:157).[106] The Koran's denial of the Lord's Crucifixion places it in opposition to the Good News that the Gospel writers announced: it disputes that He paid the price for our sins, it ignores His gift of everlasting life to those who believe on Him, it disregards His mission and purpose for coming to earth.

Next, in the verse that immediately follows, the Koran goes on to deny the Lord's Resurrection: "nay, God raised him up unto Himself" (Surah 4:158).[107] Here, the Father raises Him like Elijah: Christ was not crucified, but raised into Heaven like another prophet and mere mortal, Elijah.

Not only does the Koran continually reiterate its denial of the Sonship of Christ, it even goes a step further: it prescribes "painful chastisement" as a punishment for Christians precisely because they do embrace the Holy Trinity: "Unbelievers are those that say: 'God is one of three.' There is but one God. If they do not desist from so saying, those of them that disbelieve shall be sternly punished" (Surah 5:73).[108] This passage condones the religious persecution of those who embrace the Holy Trinity.

We hope that this brief sketch of the Koran's blasphemy of God the Father, its denial of the Holy Trinity, and its reiterative and obsessive contempt for Christ, sheds light on the spiritual and philosophical reasons for the desecration of the Church of the Nativity in Bethlehem. In Dec. 1995 Ms. Arafat placed her baby on silver star marking the site of the Lord's birthplace and knelt in mock prayer in front of the baby; violence escalated; in October 1996 the icon overlooking the site began shedding tears of blood; violence gradually and continually escalated until it reached a crescendo: by April 2002 gunmen forcibly occupied the Church and desecrated it with feces and urine for 38 days, leaving explosive devices behind when they left.

THE WEEPING ICON OF CYPRUS

<u>Date:</u> February 1, 1997
<u>Place:</u> Kykko Monastery, Cyprus
<u>Authenticated by:</u>
      Archbishop Chrysostomos, Primate of the Orthodox
      Church of Cyprus

On February 1, 1997 the holy icon "The Virgin of the Elikion" began to weep in the 11th century monastery in Kykkos, Cyprus. The monastery is located in the mountains of Cyprus 60 miles southwest of the capital, Nicosia. The icon, which portrays Mary and the Infant Jesus, was painted in the 15th century and was transferred to Kykko monastery in 1789, according to an inscription that the icon itself bears, after its original monastery was destroyed.

By February 7 the *Cyprus News Agency* reported that thousands of pilgrims had visited the monastery to see the miraculous icon and that the "15th century icon of the Virgin and the Christ-child has been shedding what seems to be thick, fragrant tears non-stop for almost a week now."[109]

Archimandrite Sergios Kykkiotis, an elder monk at the monastery, declared, "We see this as a miracle. From the way it happened, we consider it a miracle. Nothing less, nothing more…Most people go there out of curiosity but leave overwhelmed by the event. The curiosity leaves and the miracle takes over. They accept it as a miracle."[110] The miracle was authenticated by Archbishop Chrysostomos, Primate of the Orthodox Church of Cyprus.

George Philotheou, an archeologist with the Antiquities Department in Cyprus, admitted, "We can't explain it, not within any logical framework. When you are dealing with metaphysical matter, science is pretty much helpless. This was the case with similar occurrences in the past."[111]

The *Cyprus New Agency* described the consistency and fragrance of the tears thus:

> The tears are a thick, running liquid, somewhat like the sap of a pine tree. They do not evaporate, but rather remain as streaks running from the eyes of both the Virgin and the Christ-child.

"The tears have an indescribable smell which only those who concern themselves with religious matters can understand," Kykkotis says.

Other tear-shedding icons in the past have given off a similar smell, as well as the remains of saints like Saint Demetrios…

"It's a very strange smell, what we in the church call the 'evodia,'" he says.[112]

Evodia is a genus of Asiatic and Australiasian shrubs and trees (family *Rutaceæ*) that have aromatic leaves and dry fruits.

By February 10 the *New York Times* reported that more than 20,000 Cypriots had made the pilgrimage to the Kyokko Monastery to see the miraculous icon. The newspaper remarked that both Mary and Jesus in the portrait were weeping.[113]

AN ICON CARD GUSHES OIL

Date: May 10, 1997, the eve of Mother's Day
Place: the home of Sam and Salwa Najjar, Schiller Park , IL
Authenticated by:
      Bishop Demetri of the Antiochian Archdiocese

On May 10, 1997, significantly, the night before Mother's Day, an image of the Virgin Mary, with her arms extended wide open, formed by condensation in the glass of a bay window at the home of the Najjars. Sam Najjar, his wife, Salwa, and his mother were seated in the living room. Salwa noticed the image in the glass and said that she thought that the figure resembled Mary.

The following day, Mother's Day, a much greater and more astounding event occurred. Someone placed an icon card with a picture of Mary from St. George Albanian Orthodox Church on the glass and the icon card started to gush oil. The *Chicago Tribune*, in a front page story, relates the happening thus:

> On Mother's Day, the day after the Najjars saw the image of Mary on the window, the shape started dripping oil. The family has a printed card with a picture of the Miraculous Mary icon from St. George's in Cicero. A relative wanted to pray for a sick friend, so she lit a candle and put the icon card on the window where the image's head was. The card began to gush liquid down the window, Sam Najjar said.
>
> The family collected the oil in a bowl until their priest, Father Dahdal, visited on May 14. The priest put the picture in the bowl and tried to wipe the oil off the window, but it didn't go away, Sam Najjar said. The next morning, a new image of Mary had formed on the window, this time a head and torso made of oil instead of condensation, he said. The image is framed by condensation, which changes locations around Mary, he said.
>
> The picture of the Mary icon is in a bowl in a glass aquarium, surrounded by lit candles and flowers, in front of the window image. Even though some of the oil has been removed by the priest and bishop, the bowl keeps filling with oil, Sam Najjar said.[114]

On Tuesday, May 20, Bishop Demetri, of the Antiochian Archdiocese, flew to Chicago from Toledo to visit the Najjars in their Schiller Park home. He prayed in front of the window, discussed the occurrence with the family and declared the miracle to be genuine. He found that the miracle was genuine in its own right and, in addition, that it was a continuation of the miraculous icon of St. George Antiochian Orthodox Church in Cicero because it was an icon card from that church, when placed on the window, that started gushing oil.

Rev. Demetri explained the purpose of miracles:

"Miracles are done by God to teach us and to encourage us and to strengthen our faith. Christianity began with miracles," he said. "We believe in miracles and we believe they happen continuously."[115]

Rev. Dahdal of St. George's told the *Chicago Tribune* that he thought that the icon card started to spurt oil for the following reason:

"This is a sign of reconciliation," Dahdal said. "It happened on Mother's Day, and Mary is considered to be our mother. Maybe she's giving us a sign to return to her son and become better people and good Christians."[116]

MIRACLES OF HEALING PERFORMED BY THE INCORRUPTIBLE RELICS OF SAINT ALEXANDER OF SVIR

Date: 1533 and again in 1997-1998
Place: Faith, Hope, and Love Chapel at the Pokrovo-Tervenichi Convent, St. Petersburg, Russia
Authenticated by:
    Alexey II, Patriarch of Moscow and All Russia

St. Alexander of Svir was a medieval monk born in the 15th century. His parents were very pious Christians, eventually became monastics, and were canonized, as well (Saint Sergius and Saint Varvara). St. Alexander, St. Sergius, and St. Varvara belong to the St. Petersburg Eparchy-that is, they are saints who had lived in the territory of the eparchy or diocese of St. Petersburg and were declared to be saints by the Russian Orthodox Church.[117] His parents are buried at the Entrance-Oyatskaya Monastery, not far from his own burial site at the Alexander Svirsky Monastery of the Holy Trinity (Svirstroy).

St. Alexander took monastic vows and lived at the Valaam Monastery for 13 years. Longing for even more solitude and a deeper relationship with the Living God, he left the Valaam Monastery to take up residence in a secluded cell on the Svir River, after which he is named. Church history indicates that he lived on herbs and maintained strict fasting: this fact would become significant in the waning years of the 20th century in the identification of his body (his teeth show little wear).

A landmark event in the life of St. Alexander occurred the day he had a miraculous vision of the Holy Trinity. In his vision God instructed him to build a monastery to the Holy Trinity at that site. Obedient to God, St. Alexander founded a monastery there in 1484. This parcel of land is situated in the northwest region of Russia and is traversed by the Svir River, after which he is named. Svirsky's community of monks practiced strict fasting, charity, and hard physical labor in a harsh geographical setting beset by frigid weather and infertile land.

When Svirsky died in 1533, he was buried beneath the floor of his monastery. It was then that a plethora of miracles first occurred at his burial site: the blind recovered their sight, the paralyzed were healed, the possessed were exorcized. Soon the monastery became renown for the miraculous healings that the saint was performing and Svirsky was so famous, he became the patron saint of the Russian czars. Ivan the Terrible dedicated part of St. Basil, the famous onion domed cathedral on Red Square in Moscow, to Svirsky.

Three churches were built on the site: the Church of the Protecting Veil (1536), the Cathedral of the Transfiguration (1644), and the Cathedral of the Trinity (1695). This last one houses ancient frescoes. The monastery has opened its gates to tourists and visitors can examine the monastery buildings and the three churches on the site. A pine forest, proximity to the Svir river, and two large lakes provide an idyllic, picturesque atmosphere to the cloistral landscape.

Although St. Alexander was venerated down through the centuries and Svirstroy attracted pilgrims who were suffering from debilitating diseases and were in search of a miracle of healing, everything changed with the Communist Revolution. When the Bolsheviks seized power in 1917, they set out to crush all religious belief. Svirsky's body disappeared, along with those of 62 other saints. It was not until after the fall of the Soviet Union that it was found.

In 1991 Father Lukian Kutsenko set out to restore the Svirsky Monastery and the nearby Pokrovo (Protection)-Tervenichi Convent. In 1997 Father Lukian entrusted Sister Leonida Safonova of the Convent, who was formerly a biologist, with the task of conducting research and finding Svirsky's body. Sister Leonida began her investigation by examining Bolshivik archives. The *Chicago Tribune* describes the great discovery that Sister Leonida made thus:

Leonida's search of Bolshevik archives unearthed an entry describing an examination of Svirsky's remains by scientists in 1919. That led to the Military Medical Academy, a cavernous institution where among meticulously cataloged skeletons, skulls and preserved organs she discovered a corpse wrapped in sheets without a number or identification tag that had been kept as an example of "natural mummification."

Though lacking identifying clothing, the mummy's feet were crossed in the way described in medieval writings about the saint. The face, she said, though devoid of hair and beard, resembled the monk's likeness in icons painted while he lived.

The right fingers were damaged, which Leonida took as evidence that priests, in a common practice then, had harvested bits of his fingers for veneration as relics. The corpse, especially its legs, periodically oozed droplets of a fragrant, clear liquid.[118]

The relics of St. Alexander are truly miraculous, as there is not a single indication of decomposition to be found anywhere on his body. The facial features, which, under normal circumstances are usually the first to disappear, are perfectly preserved-the lips, nose, and ears are whole; the facial skin is soft and moist, not shrunken at all; the skin is an amber yellow, the scent of myrrh and heavenly sweet scents emanate.

Sister Leonida drove the mummy to the Faith, Hope, and Love Chapel at her convent and laid it out on a bier for the faithful to venerate. It was then that an outpouring of miracles began and did not cease. The *Chicago Tribune* reports:

> Then the miracles started. "There were so many we stopped counting," Leonida said. "There was a woman whose 5-year-old daughter had a central nervous system disease. She couldn't walk, speak or hear. By the third visit, she was walking, like a toddler, from the church. Everyone was crying."

> When the head of the Russian Orthodox Church, Patriarch Alexey II, visited the tiny church last summer to venerate the remains, it was official: in the eyes of the church, this was Svirsky.[119]

In December 1998 St. Alexander Svirsky's body was returned, at long last, to the monastery that he had founded. However, miracles are still reported in the convent's little chapel in St. Petersburg. Faith the size of a mustard seed is powerful, as Christ instructed (Mat 17:20; Luke 17:6), and the Saint is continuing to watch over his flock.

Endnotes

1   Irenaeus, *Irenaeus against Heresies*, 3.19.1, in *The Apostolic Fathers with Justin Martyr, Irenaeus*, vol. 1 of *Ante-Nicene Fathers*, edited by Alexander Roberts and James Donaldson (New York: The Christian Literature Company, 1890-1897), 448-49 [Irenaeus, *Contra hæreses*, 3.19.1, in Jacques-Paul Migne, ed., *Patrologiæ cursos completus...Series græca*, 161 vols. (Paris: Migne, 1857-1866), 7:938C-940A].

2   Athanasius, *On the Incarnation of the Word of God*, 54.3, in *Athanasius: Select Works and Letters*, vol. 4 of *Nicene and Post-Nicene Fathers of the Christian Church*, 2nd series, edited by Philip Schaff and Henry Wace (New York: Christian Literature Publishing Company, 1890-1900), 65 [Athanasius, *Oratio de Incarnatione Verbi*, 54.3, in Jacques-Paul Migne, ed., *Patrologiæ cursos completus... Series græca*, 161 vols. (Paris: Migne, 1857-1866), 25:192B].

3   Irenaeus, *Irenaeus against Heresies*, 3.17-19, in *The Apostolic Fathers with Justin Martyr, Irenaeus*, vol. 1 of *Ante-Nicene Fathers*, edited by Alexander Roberts and James Donaldson (New York: The Christian Literature Company, 1890-1897), 444-49 [Irenaeus, *Contra hæreses*, 3.17-19, in Jacques-Paul Migne, ed., *Patrologiæ cursos completus...Series græca*, 161 vols. (Paris: Migne, 1857-1866), 7:929B-941C].

4   Athanasius, *Against the Arians*, 2.59, in *Athanasius: Select Works and Letters*, vol. 4 of *Nicene and Post-Nicene Fathers of the Christian Church*, 2nd series, edited by Philip Schaff and Henry Wace (New York: Christian Literature Publishing Company, 1890-1900), 380-81 [Athanasius, *Oratio II contra Arianos*, 2.59, in Jacques-Paul Migne, ed., *Patrologiæ cursos completus...Series græca*, 161 vols. (Paris: Migne, 1857-1866), 26:272B-273C].

5   Cyril of Alexandria, *Commentary on the Gospel according to S. John*, John 1:13-14, 2 vols., translated by Thomas Randell, preface by H.P. Liddon (London: Walter Smith, 1885), 2:105-12 [Cyril of

Alexandria, *In Joannis Evangelium Lib. I*, Joannes 1:13-14, in Jacques-Paul Migne, ed., *Patrologiæ cursos completus...Series græca*, 161 vols. (Paris: Migne, 1857-1866), 73:153D-165B].

6   John Chrysostom, *Homilies on the Gospel of St. John*, John 1:14, in *Saint Chrysostom: Homilies on the Gospel of St. John and the Epistle to the Hebrews*, vol. 14 of *Nicene and Post-Nicene Fathers of the Christian Church*, 2nd series, edited by Philip Schaff and Henry Wace (New York: Christian Literature Publishing Company, 1890-1900), 38 [John Chrysostom, *In Joannem homiliæ*, Joannes 1:14, in Jacques-Paul Migne, ed., *Patrologiæ cursos completus... Series græca*, 161 vols. (Paris: Migne, 1857-1866), 59:77-86].

7   Peter Chrysologus, *Sermons*, 67; 70, on the Lord's Prayer, in *Saint Peter Chrysologus: Selected Sermons; and Saint Valerian: Homilies*, translated by George E. Ganss (New York: Fathers of the Church, Inc., 1953), 115-123; Peter Chrysologus, *Sermons on the Lord's Prayer*, 68.3; 71.2-3; 72.3, in *St. Peter Chrysologus: Selected Sermons*, translated by William B. Palardy, vol. 2 (Washington, DC: Catholic University of America Press, 2004), 276, 285-87, 293 [Peter Chrysologus, *Sermones in orationem Dominicam*, 67, 68.3, 70, 71.2-3, 72.3, in Jacques-Paul Migne, ed., *Patrologiæ cursos completus...Series latina*, 221 vols. (Paris: Migne, 1844-1879), 52:390-93, 394C-395A, 398C-401A, 401B-402A, 404C-405C].

8   Macarius of Egypt, *Makarian Homilies* 4.67 and 6.124 (in *Philokalia*, 3:314, 330); Chrysostom *Homilies on Ephesians* 20 (Eph 5:22-33).

9   Ilas the Presbyter, *Gnomic Anthology* 3.25 (in *Philokalia*, 3:50)

10   Daniel B. Clendenin, *Eastern Orthodox Christianity: A Western Perspective*, 2nd ed. (Grand Rapids: Baker Academic, 2005), 126-27.

11   Metropolitan Philaret, "Homily 12," in *Complete Works* (in Russian) (Moscow, 1873), 99.

12   Giovan Domenico Mansi, Sixth Session, in *Sacrorum conciliorum nova, et amplissima collectio...*, 53 vol. (Florence: Antonio Zatta, 1759-1927), 12:321CD.

13   Irina Gorainoff, *Séraphim de Sarov* (Bégrolles-en-Mauges: Abbaye de Bellefontaine, 1973), 208-14.

14   Leonid Ouspensky, "The Meaning and Content of the Icon," *Theology of the Icon*, translated by Anthony Gythiel with selections translated by Elizabeth Meyendorff, 2 vols (Crestwood: St. Vladimir's Seminary Press, 1992), 1:151-94, reprinted in Daniel B. Clendenin, ed., *Eastern Orthodox Theology: A Contemporary Reader*, 2nd ed. (Grand Rapids: Baker Academic, 2004), 33-63.

15   Ibid., 43.

16   Ibid.

17 John of Damascus, *Apologia of St. John Damascene against Those who Decry Holy Images*, Part 3, in *St. John Damascene on Holy Images; Followed by Three Sermons on the Assumption*, translated by Mary H. Allies (London: Thomas Baker, 1898), 129-30. John of Damascus, in *De Imaginibus Oratio III*, in Jacques-Paul Migne, ed., *Patrologiæ cursos completus...Series græca*, 161 vols. (Paris: Migne, 1857-1866), 94:1384D.

18 Ibid., Part 1, 47-48. John of Damascus, in *De Imaginibus Oratio I*, in Jacques-Paul Migne, ed., *Patrologiæ cursos completus...Series græca*, 161 vols. (Paris: Migne, 1857-1866), 94:1276A.

19 Ibid., 15-16. [Ibid., 94:1245A].

20 John Baggley, *Doors of Perception: Icons and their Spiritual Significance* (London: Mowbray, 1987).

21 Daniel B. Clendenin, *Eastern Orthodox Christianity: A Western Perspective*, 2nd ed. (Grand Rapids: Baker Academic, 2005), 37, 43, 71-93, 95, 100, 110, 115, 152-55, 174.

22 Daniel B. Clendenin, *Eastern Orthodox Theology: A Contemporary Reader*, 2nd ed. (Grand Rapids: Baker Academic, 2004), 17-19, 33-63, 73, 90, 132, 145-46, 150, 265.

23 Paul Evdokimov, *The Art of the Icon: A Theology of Beauty* (Torrance: Oakwood, 1990).

24 St. John of Damascus, *On the Divine Images: Three Apologies against Those Who Attack the Divine Images*, translated by David Anderson (Crestwood: St. Vladimir's Seminary Press, 1980).

25 Leonid Ouspensky, *Theology of the Icon*, translated by Anthony Gythiel with selections translated by Elizabeth Meyendorff, 2 vols. (Crestwood: St. Vladimir's Seminary Press, 1992).

26 Leonid Ouspensky and Vladimir Lossky, *The Meaning of Icons*, translated by G.E.H. Palmer and E. Kadloubovsky, rev. ed. (Crestwood: St. Vladimir's Seminary Press, 1982).

27 Jaroslav Pelikan, *Imago Dei: The Byzantine Apologia for Icons* (Washington, DC: National Gallery of Art; Princeton: Princeton University Press, 1990).

28 Michel Quenot, *The Icon: Window on the Kingdom*, translated by a Carthusian monk (Crestwood: St. Vladimir's Seminary Press, 1991).

29 Daniel J. Sahas, *Icon and Logos: Sources in Eighth-Century Iconoclasm* (Toronto: University of Toronto Press, 1986).

30 Egon Sendler, *The Icon, Image of the Invisible: Elements of Theology, Aesthetics and Technique*, translated by Fr. Steven Bigham (Redondo Beach: Oakwood Publications, 1988).

31 St. Theodore of Studites, *St. Theodore of Studites on the Holy Icons*, translated by Catharine Roth (Crestwood: St. Vladimir's Seminary Press, 1981).

32 Bishop Kallistos Ware, *The Orthodox Way* (Crestwood: St. Vladimir's Seminary Press, 1995), 54, 72, 120.

33 Timothy Ware, *The Orthodox Church*, rev. ed. (London: Penguin Books, 1997), 30-34, 41, 47, 84, 86, 97, 99, 122, 141-42, 148-49, 179, 201, 206, 218-19, 221, 231, 233n1, 256, 270-72,

34 Sergius Bulgakov, *The Orthodox Church*, rev. ed. (Crestwood: St. Vladimir's Seminary Press, 1988), 129.

35 John of Damascus, *On Divine Images*, 1.17; 2.14 (Crestwood: St. Vladimir's Seminary Press, 1980); see also the commentary, p. 39.

36 Daniel B. Clendenin, *Eastern Orthodox Christianity: A Western Perspective*, 2nd ed. (Grand Rapids: Baker Academic, 2005), 72-73.

37 Sergius Bulgakov, "The Orthodox Church," in James Pain and Nicolas Zernov, eds., *A Bulgakov Anthology* (Philadelphia: Westminster Press, 1976), 12.

38 Thomas Doulis, ed., *Journeys to Orthodoxy: A Collection of Essays by Converts to Orthodox Christianity* (Minneapolis: Light and Life, 1986); see also James J. Stamoolis, *Eastern Orthodox Mission Theology Today* (Maryknoll: Orbis Books, 1986), 99.

39 Daniel B. Clendenin, *Eastern Orthodox Christianity: A Western Perspective*, 2nd ed. (Grand Rapids: Baker Academic, 2005), 74. Regarding Orthodoxy's involvement of the five senses, Clendenin cites the following sources: Michel Quenot, *The Icon: Window on the Kingdom* (Crestwood: St. Vladimir's Seminary Press, 1991), 47; Jaroslav Pelikan, *Imago Dei: The Byzantine Apologia for icons* (Princeton: Princeton University Press, 1990), 108-11; Nicodemos of Athos, *Handbook of Spiritual Counsel* (New York: Paulist, 1989), chaps. 3-8; John of Damascus, *Exposition of the Orthodox Faith*, 2.18 ("Concerning Sense Perception") and *Divine Images*, 1.16-17.

40 Sergius Bulgakov, "The Virgin and the Saints in Orthodoxy," *The Orthodox Church* (Crestwood: St. Vladimir's Seminary Press, 1988), 116-28, reprinted in Daniel B. Clendenin, *Eastern Orthodox Theology: A Contemporary Reader*, 2nd ed. (Grand Rapids: Baker Academic, 2004), 65-75.

41 Sergius Bulgakov, "The Virgin and the Saints in Orthodoxy," in *The Orthodox Church* (Crestwood: St. Vladimir's Seminary Press, 1988), 116-28, reprinted in Daniel B. Clendenin, *Eastern Orthodox Theology: A Contemporary Reader*, 2nd ed. (Grand Rapids: Baker Academic, 2004), 65-75.

42 Timothy Ware, *The Orthodox Church*, rev. ed (London: Penguin Books, 1997), 258-59.

43 Ibid., 260.

44 *The Passing of Mary: Second Latin Form*, in *The Twelve Patriarchs, Excerpts and Epistles, The Clementina, Apocrypha, Decretals,*

Memoirs of Edessa and Syriac Documents, Remains of the First Ages, vol. 8 of *Ante-Nicene Fathers*, edited by Alexander Roberts and James Donaldson (New York: The Christian Literature Company, 1890-1897), 595-98.

45 John of Damascus, *Three Sermons on the Dormition of the Virgin*, Sermon 2, in *St. John Damascene on Holy Images; Followed by Three Sermons on the Assumption*, translated by Mary H. Allies (London: Thomas Baker, 1898), 195-96.

46 *The Departure of My Lady Mary from this World*, in Benjamin Harris Cowper, ed., *The Journal of Sacred Literature and Biblical Record* 7, no. 13 (April 1865):129-60.

47 John the Theologian, *The Book of John concerning the Falling Asleep of Mary*, in *The Twelve Patriarchs, Excerpts and Epistles, The Clementina, Apocrypha, Decretals, Memoirs of Edessa and Syriac Documents, Remains of the First Ages*, vol. 8 of *Ante-Nicene Fathers*, edited by Alexander Roberts and James Donaldson (New York: The Christian Literature Company, 1890-1897), 587-91.

48 *The Passing of Mary: First Latin Form*, in *The Twelve Patriarchs, Excerpts and Epistles, The Clementina, Apocrypha, Decretals, Memoirs of Edessa and Syriac Documents, Remains of the First Ages*, vol. 8 of *Ante-Nicene Fathers*, edited by Alexander Roberts and James Donaldson (New York: The Christian Literature Company, 1890-1897), 592-94.

49 *The Passing of Mary: Second Latin Form*, in *The Twelve Patriarchs, Excerpts and Epistles, The Clementina, Apocrypha, Decretals, Memoirs of Edessa and Syriac Documents, Remains of the First Ages*, vol. 8 of *Ante-Nicene Fathers*, edited by Alexander Roberts and James Donaldson (New York: The Christian Literature Company, 1890-1897), 595-98.

50 Cyril of Jerusalem, *Discourse on Mary Theotokos*, in *Miscellaneous Coptic Texts in the Dialect of Upper Egypt*, translated by E.A.Wallis Budge (London: British Museum, 1915), 626-50.

51 Evodius, *The Falling Asleep of Mary*, in *Coptic Apocryphal Gospels: Translations Together with the Texts of Some of Them*, translated by Forbes Robinson (Cambridge: University Press, 1896), 44-67.

52 Theodosius of Alexandria, *The Falling Asleep of Mary*, in *Coptic Apocryphal Gospels: Translations Together with the Texts of Some of Them*, translated by Forbes Robinson (Cambridge: University Press, 1896), 90-127.

53 John of Damascus, *Three Sermons on the Dormition of the Virgin*, in *St. John Damascene on Holy Images; Followed by Three Sermons on the Assumption*, translated by Mary H. Allies (London: Thomas Baker, 1898), 147-211.

54 *Munificentissimus Deus*, 40; 44, http://www.ewtn.com/library/ PAPALDOC/P12MUNIF.HTM (November 2, 2007).

55 Mitchell Locin, "Weeping Icon Draws Worshipers," *Chicago Tribune*, December 9, 1986, 3.

56 Ibid.

57 Tasia Kavvadias, "Icon's Miraculous Sign Draws Multitude," *Chicago Tribune*, December 15, 1986, 1.

58 "Weeping Virgin Icon Draws Throngs to Chicago," *New York Times*, December 22, 1986, B16; "Throngs Flock to Weeping Virgin," *San Francisco Chronicle*, December 23, 1986, 12.

59 Mitchell Locin, "Visitors to Force Church to Cut Its Hours," *Chicago Tribune*, January 14, 1987, 8.

60 Bruce Buursma, "Greek Orthodox Leader Calls Weeping Madonna Icon a Sign, not a Miracle," *Chicago Tribune*, February 11, 1987, 3.

61 Jessica Seigel, "Faithful Gather to See Icon's Tears," *Chicago Tribune*, September 11, 1988, 3.

62 Timothy Ware, *The Orthodox Church*, rev. ed. (London: Penguin Books, 1997), 12.

63 Ibid., 145-46, 148. Ware derives the number of martyr-bishops under Bolshevik rule from Nikita A. Struve, *Christians in Contemporary Russia*, translated by Lancelot Sheppard and A. Manson (London: Harvill, 1967), 393-98.

64 Ibid., 151.

65 Ibid.

66 Ibid., 149.

67 Walter Kolarz, *Religion in the Soviet Union* (New York: St. Martin's Press; London: MacMillan and Company, 1961).

68 Dimitry Pospielovsky, *The Russian Church under the Soviet Regime 1917-1982*, 2 vols. (Crestwood: St. Vladimir's Seminary Press, 1984).

69 Nikita A. Struve. *Christians in Contemporary Russia*, translated by Lancelot Sheppard and A. Manson (London: Harvill, 1967).

70 Timothy Ware, *The Orthodox Church*, rev. ed. (London: Penguin Books, 1997), 11-12, 145-60.

71 Ibid., 167.

72 Daniel B. Clendenin, *Eastern Orthodox Christianity: A Western Perspective*, 2nd ed. (Grand Rapids: Baker Academic, 2005), 147.

73 Vladimir Lossky, *The Mystical Theology of the Eastern Church*, translated by members of the Fellowship of St. Albans and St. Sergius (London: J. Clarke, 1957), 245-46 [*Essai sur la théologie mystique de l'Eglise d'Orient*. Paris: Aubier, 1944]. Lossky is cited by Timothy Ware, *The Orthodox Church*, rev. ed. (London: Penguin Books, 1997), 148-49.

74 Timothy Ware, *The Orthodox Church*, rev. ed. (London: Penguin Books, 1997), 149n1.

75 Jane Arraf, "Patriarch Declares Miracle after Communion Bread Reportedly Spouts Blood," *Houston Chronicle*, April 30, 1991, 14.

76 Michael Hirsley, "Icon's Tears are Turning into a Stream of People," *Chicago Tribune*, May 6, 1994, 1.

77 St. Peter of Damaskos, "The Sixth Stage of Contemplation" in *The Philokalia: The Complete Text; Compiled by St. Nikodemus of the Holy Mountain and St. Makarius of Corinth*. Translated and edited by G.E.H. Palmer, Philip Sherrard, and Kallistos Ware, 4 vols. (London: Faber and Faber Limited, 1979-1995), 3:137.

78 Penny Roberts, "Many Find Miracle in Weeping Mary, *Chicago Tribune*, April 25, 1994, 3.

79 Eric Zorn, "Icon Is Still Crying for Our Attention," *Chicago Tribune*, May 15, 1994, 1.

80 Ibid.

81 Henri E. Cauvin, "Believers Still Flock to Cicero Icon," *Chicago Tribune*, July 15, 1991, 8.

82 Ibid.

83 Ibid.

84 www.atlastours.net/holyland/church_of_the_nativity.html (Dec. 7, 2007); www.sacred-destinations.com/israel/bethlehem_church_of_the_nativity.htm (Dec. 7, 2007).

85 Associated Press Television, untitled, November 28, 1996, http://www.aparchive.com/user/GetOneUp.aspx?id=38991&links=BLINK,JESUS,DECLAR,MIRACL,USABL&media=Text&pu=h (Dec. 7, 2007).

86 Ibid.

87 Jerrold Kessel, "Jesus Painting Said to Wink and Shed Tears in Bethlehem," www.cnn.com/ WORLD/9611/29/weeping.jesus/index.html (Dec. 7, 2007).

88 Ibid.

89 Tom Gross, "Miracle Declared in Bethlehem as Jesus Weeps," *Jerusalem Post*, November 28, 1996; Tom Gross, "Are Tears Flowing from Jesus Painting?" *Jerusalem Post Service*, December 6, 1996.

90 Karin Laub, "Blinking Jesus Declared Miracle," *Times-Picayune*, November 29, 1996, A25.

91 Serge Schmemann, "Arafat Visits Liberated Bethlehem," *Times-Picayune*, December 24, 1995, A.3.

92 Serge Schmemann, "Arafat Speaks to Throngs in Bethlehem, *New York Times*, December 24, 1995, 1.9.

93 Serge Schmemann, "In the Land of Faith, a Time for Utter Disbelief," *New York Times*, March 10, 2002, 4.1.

94 There are some excellent websites that delineate the differences between the Bible and the Koran, God and Allah. We have taken our material from the following two websites:www.answering-islam. org/Nehls/tt1/tt6.html, erichmusick.com/writings/02/researchpaper. html

95 *The Qu'ran*, translated by E.H. Palmer (Oxford: The Clarendon Press, 1900).

96 *The Meaning of the Glorious Koran; An Explanatory Translation*, translated by Mohammed Marmaduke Pickthall (New York: New American Library, 1930).

97 Ibid.

98 Ibid.

99 *The Holy Qurān; English Translation & Commentary (with Arabic Text) by A. Yūsuf Ali* (Lahore: Shaikh Muhammad Ashraf, 1934).

100 *The Meaning of the Glorious Koran; An Explanatory Translation by Mohammed Marmaduke Pickthall* (New York: New American Library, 1930).

101 *The Koran*, translated and annotated by N.J. Dawood (London: Penguin Books, 1999).

102 *The Koran; Translated from the Arabic, the Suras Arranged in Chronological Order, with Notes and Index, by J.M. Rodwell* (London: Williams and Norgate, 1861).

103 *The Meaning of the Glorious Koran; An Explanatory Translation by Mohammed Marmaduke Pickthall* (New York: New American Library, 1930).

104 Ibid.

105 Ibid.

106 Ibid.

107 *The Qu'ran*, translated by E.H. Palmer (Oxford: The Clarendon Press, 1900).

108 *The Koran*, translated and annotated by N.J. Dawood (London: Penguin Books, 1999).

109 Menelaos Hadjicostis, "Weeping Icon Moves a Nation," *Cyprus News Agency*, February 7, 2007.

110 Ibid.

111 Ibid.

112 Ibid.

113 *New York Times*, February 10, 1997.

114 Suzy Frisch, "Virgin Mary Apparition on Window Draws Faithful," *Chicago Tribune*, May 22, 1997, 1.

115 Ibid.

116 Ibid.

117 An eparch is a bishop of the Eastern Orthodox Church; an eparchy is a diocese.

118 Elizabeth Williamson, "Russian Faithful Turn to Mummy at a Time of Great Stress, Discovery of a Monk's Suspected Remains Has Been Proclaimed a Miracle," *Chicago Tribune*, January 3, 1999, 5.

119 Ibid.

CONCLUSION

But seek ye first the kingdom of God, and his righteousness;
and all these things shall be added unto you.

—Mat 6:33

Researching this book has changed my life forever and I hope that reading it has enriched yours. The biographies of St. Herman of Alaska, St. Seraphim of Sarov, St. Alexander of Svir, the monks on Mt. Athos, and the countless other saints who have given their lives to Christ down through the centuries, indicate that when people make the choice to follow Christ first and to forsake everything else, they acquire a brand new identity in Him-they see clearly that image, education, career, the approval of others, and money, are graven images that do not bring everlasting life. Image, approval, and money are particularly harsh taskmasters that always demand more sacrifice. In addition, I have been deeply moved by Patriarch Diodorus I, the Greek Orthodox Patriarch of Jerusalem, who has said that the Miracle of the Holy Flame reminds him that Heaven is very near.

— Mary Efrosini Gregory —

In my previous book, *An Eastern Orthodox View of Pascal,* I began my exploration of Christianity by researching the brilliant proofs that Blaise Pascal had devised to demonstrate that God exists. To be sure, Pascal did provide mathematical, rational, empirical proof of His existence. Pascal's first proof is that the fact that one person has fulfilled hundreds of biblical prophecies is beyond the realm of statistical probability: it provides evidence as to the existence of Divine Will. He posited that in the seventeenth century. Since then, many others have added to his thesis and have concretized it. For example, Peter W. Stoner, in *Science Speaks,* has calculated that the statistical probability that one man would fulfill just 8 Messianic prophecies is $1:10^{17}$, that is, 1 in 1 followed by 17 zeroes.[1] Furthermore, Stoner has also calculated that the chances that one person would fulfill 48 biblical prophecies is $1:10^{157}$, or 1 in 1 followed by 157 zeroes![2] Moreover, in 1883 Alfred Edersheim, in *The Life and Times of Jesus the Messiah,* appendix 9, identified and enumerated 456 Messianic prophecies that Christ fulfilled![3] Edersheim's work is the result of having carefully scrutinized over 8,000 verses of Bible prophecy. The fact that one man has fulfilled 456 Messianic prophecies is not the result of random chance, it points to Divine Will.

Another proof that Pascal offers of God's existence is miracles. Miracles provide empirical proof of a realm that is invisible to the naked eye. Hence, knowing that the Orthodox Church, the True Church of Jesus Christ on earth, His faithful bride, is rich in miracles, I set out to count as many as I could. First, I was overwhelmed by the sheer number that have occurred over two millennia. However, then I was even more astounded by the lives of the holy men and women whom God had chosen to be vehicles for His miracles.

I am particularly struck and forever changed by the life of St. Seraphim of Sarov. He was brutally beaten by thieves with the handle of his own axe, left permanently crippled, had to walk, hunched over with a cane the remainder of his life, and yet, when his assailants were apprehended, he pleaded for their forgiveness before a judge. Now, how many people would do that? How many souls can find the generosity to forgive that? No wonder God loved him!

The Holy Spirit made Himself manifest in St. Seraphim. The Saint could read the thoughts of others and advise them in an intensely personal way, giving them information that applied only to them and to no one else. Wild animals became tame and ate out of his hands! And, of course, his transfiguration into a being of dazzling, bright light teaches Christian seekers many things. First, the Holy Spirit, does, indeed, manifest Himself in His saints for the glorification of God and the education of humans. Secondly, the miracle provides physical proof of the existence of God. Thirdly, we understand precisely how to do the will of God to the point that the Holy Spirit would manifest Himself in the form of blinding light. The commandment is to seek first the Kingdom of Heaven and then everything else will follow.

I wrote my previous book, *An Eastern Orthodox View of Pascal*, with the objective of bringing the Good News of the Risen Christ to atheist academia. Since it is a scholarly work, university libraries will purchase it, and hopefully, skeptics, who have only half the story of creation, that of the physical realm, may read it, believe, and receive the precious gift of everlasting life.

Then I set out to investigate the miracles of the Orthodox Church. Orthodoxy has remained faithful to Christ throughout the centuries, and He has indeed, opened His Heart and blessed the Church abundantly. Moreover, Christ must have been praying for the Orthodox Church because, unlike the West, it has remained whole and unfragmented for two thousand years. Conversely, the West has been sifted like grains of flour into countless churches and denominations. One is reminded of

Christ's words to Peter that He has prayed for him so that he would not be sifted like wheat (Luke 22:31; 1 Pet 5:8).

What strikes me is what it takes to follow Christ to the point that one has the ability to manifest the Holy Spirit as Seraphim had done. First, one cannot love any of the graven images that are commonly worshipped today-image, education, career, the approval of others, or money. This last one, the love of money, is a particularly tough one to renounce. Next, one cannot be too comfortable. The Laodiceans were too comfortable, self-satisfied, and apathetic, and Christ reprimanded them (Rev 3:14-18). Next, one has to announce the truth to the world. That one means taking chances. Telling the truth can be dangerous in any country. A particularly tough assignment is forgiving one's attackers, even if they are brutal.

It becomes evident that Christ came to lift us out of our animalistic, evolutionary underpinnings-concern only for self, survival, family, tribe, comfort; not to mention giving in to one's impulses. His message was the opposite-concern for others, embracing death, self-denial; becoming dead to one's impulses. This age is the time to rise up beyond our animal origins. We could never accomplish this without Christ having come to earth. He spoke with authority and explained exactly what it takes to follow Him. St. Seraphim and countless other saints have taken Him up on His challenge. The miracles that the saints have performed provide evidence that this life is not all that there is, that Christ does give everlasting life to those who believe in Him, and that if we are strong-willed enough to take Him up on His challenge, we, too, may one day perform miracles. The key is to seek first the Kingdom of Heaven, and then everything else will follow.

One last word for any skeptics who may have tripped across this book in the semi-illuminated stacks of a university library and have opened it up out of curiosity. I know that people who are pressed for time tend to speed-read and check out the conclusion first. Now, slow down, and read this very, very slowly: skeptics who take pride in their intellectual capabilities and rational thinking processes say that they would like to believe, but they must reject anything that is not based on reason and empiricism. We recommend that they get on a plane and visit the Church of the Resurrection in Jerusalem on Orthodox Holy Saturday to be present for the Miracle of the Holy Flame. This miracle has been documented by the French monk Bernard in 870 AD and Abbot Daniel of Tchernigov in 1106-7 AD. Multitudes of Orthodox Christians make a pilgrimage to the Church every year to be present for the Miracle. They post photographs and personal accounts of the Miracle all over the Internet. The Tomb of Christ is the place where Heaven meets earth. This is where the seen and the unseen worlds intersect. If the unseen world were to exist, wouldn't you want to be the first to know? Wouldn't you demand empirical evidence? Well, here it is.

Yes, this plane ride to the Church of the Resurrection on Orthodox Holy Saturday would be a good idea for you intellectuals who admit that the more that you learn about science, the more it is that you realize that you do not know; you, who admit that as you detect smaller and smaller particles, you realize that there is more and more that you cannot detect. Yes, you astrophysicists who have figured out that the universe is expanding at an accelerating rate, but do not know why. Yes, you quantum physicists who posit that subatomic particles must be everywhere at the same time. Your math and science take you as far back as the Big Bang, but no further. You cannot see beyond this universe. You cannot calculate what happened before creation. So, how do you know that there is not One who antecedes time and space? How do you explain the fact that Stoner has calculated that the statistical probability that one man would fulfill just 8 Messianic prophecies is $1:10^{17}$, that the chances that one person would fulfill 48 biblical prophecies is $1:10^{157}$, and that yet it happened?[4] How do you explain the fact that Edersheim identified and enumerated 456 Messianic prophecies that Christ fulfilled?[5] Can you even calculate the statistical probability that one man would fulfill 456 prophecies? Well, don't bother, you don't have to: even without the math, one must necessarily extrapolate that the fact that one man has fulfilled 456 Messianic prophecies is not the result of random chance, it points to Divine Will.

Researching this book has taught me that God is very near and that He is always watching over man. The writings of the monks on Mount Athos and other saints who have sacrificed everything to follow Christ indicate that those who are pure in heart do, indeed, see God and that those who, like Moses, have an ongoing relationship with Him, can depend on Him. Miracles, then, are evidence of a relationship between God and man. Belief is the first step that man takes on a ladder leading towards theosis. As men strive to purify their hearts, miracles do happen and are part of the deepening friendship between man and God.

The first miracle that happens is the change of heart that takes place in the believer. Those who give their hearts to Christ suddenly see the things of the world as they really are: ephemeral, false, enslaving, deceiving. The fact that many nations living in darkness left their pagan practices to lead a holy life with Christ as their King is a miracle. The fact that cowards became brave and willing to be martyred for the Risen Lord is a miracle. Truth replaced the lie of paganism. The King of Heaven and earth replaced the deceiver of the world in the hearts of many. Men found strength within themselves to turn over a new page and seek the things that belong to God. The fact that a fledgling religion, despite great persecution, has swept the face of the earth and changed it forever, is proof that once man gets the flame of a new friendship between the Living God and himself started, miracles do happen.

Endnotes

1   Peter W. Stoner, *Science Speaks* (Chicago: Moody Press, 1958). This book is available online at http://www.geocities.com/stonerdon/ science_speaks.html (February 14, 2007).

2   Ibid.

3   Alfred Edersheim, *The Life and Times of Jesus the Messiah* (New York: Anson D.F. Randolph, 1883), appendix 9, 707-38.

4   Peter W. Stoner, *Science Speaks* (Chicago: Moody Press, 1958). This book is available online at http://www.geocities.com/stonerdon/ science_speaks.html (February 14, 2007).

5   Alfred Edersheim, *The Life and Times of Jesus the Messiah* (New York: Anson D.F. Randolph, 1883), appendix 9, 707-38.

BIBLIOGRAPHY

PRIMARY SOURCES

Athanasius, Saint. *Against the Arians* in *Athanasius: Select Works and Letters*. Vol. 4 of *Nicene and Post-Nicene Fathers of the Christian Church*. 2nd series. Edited by Philip Schaff and Henry Wace. New York: Christian Literature Publishing Company, 1890-1900.

_____. *On the Incarnation of the Word of God* in *Athanasius: Select Works and Letters*. Vol. 4 of *Nicene and Post-Nicene Fathers of the Christian Church*. 2nd series. Edited by Philip Schaff and Henry Wace. New York: Christian Literature Publishing Company, 1890-1900.

Cyril of Alexandria, Saint. *Commentary on the Gospel according to S. John*. Vol. 2. Translated by Thomas Randell. Preface by H.P. Liddon. London: Walter Smith, 1885.

Cyril of Jerusalem, Saint. *Discourse on Mary Theotokos* in *Miscellaneous Coptic Texts in the Dialect of Upper Egypt*. Translated by E.A. Wallis Budge. London: British Museum, 1915, 626-50.

The Departure of My Lady Mary from this World, in Benjamin
Harris Cowper, ed., *The Journal of Sacred Literature and
Biblical Record* 7, no. 3 (April 1865):129-60.

Evodius, Saint. *The Falling Asleep of Mary* in *Coptic Apocryphal
Gospels: Translations Together with the Texts of Some of
Them*. Translated by Forbes Robinson. Cambridge:
University Press, 1896, 44-67.

*The Holy Qurān; English Translation & Commentary (with Arabic
Text) by A. Yūsuf Ali*. Lahore: Shaikh Muhammad Ashraf,
1934.

Irenaeus, Saint. *Irenaeus against Heresies* in *The Apostolic Fathers
with Justin Martyr, Irenaeus*. Vol. 1 of *Ante-Nicene Fathers*.
Edited by Alexander Roberts and James Donaldson. New
York: The Christian Literature Company, 1890-1897.

John Chrysostom, Saint. *Homilies on the Gospel of St. John* in
*Saint Chrysostom: Homilies on the Gospel of St. John and the
Epistle to the Hebrews*. Vol. 14 of *Nicene and Post-Nicene
Fathers of the Christian Church*. 2nd series. Edited by Philip
Schaff and Henry Wace. New York: Christian Literature
Publishing Company, 1890-1900.

John of Damascus, Saint. *On the Divine Images: Three Apologies
against Those Who Attack the Divine Images*. Translated by
David Anderson. Crestwood: St. Vladimir's Seminary
Press, 1980.

_____. *Apologia of St. John Damascene against Those who Decry
Holy Images* in *St. John Damascene on Holy Images; Followed
by Three Sermons on the Assumption*. Translated by Mary
H. Allies. London: Thomas Baker, 1898, 1-145.

_____. *Three Sermons on the Dormition of the Virgin* in *St. John
Damascene on Holy Images: Followed by Three Sermons on
the Assumption*. Translated by Mary H. Allies. London:
Thomas Baker, 1898, 147-211.

John the Theologian, Saint. *The Book of John concerning the Falling
Asleep of Mary* in *The Twelve Patriarchs, Excerpts and
Epistles, The Clementina, Apocrypha, Decretals, Memoirs of*

Edessa and Syriac Documents, Remains of the First Ages. Vol. 8 of *Ante-Nicene Fathers.* Edited by Alexander Roberts and James Donaldson. New York: The Christian Literature Company, 1890-1897, 587-91.

The Koran. Translated and annotated by N.J. Dawood. London: Penguin Books, 1999.

The Koran; Translated from the Arabic, the Suras Arranged in Chronological Order, with Notes and Index, by J.M. Rodwell. London: Williams and Norgate, 1861.

Mansi, Giovan Domenico. *Sacrorum conciliorum nova, et amplissima collectio* 53 vols. Florence: Antonio Zatta, 1759-1927.

The Meaning of the Glorious Koran: An Explanatory Translation. Translated by Mohammed Marmaduke Pickthall. New York: New American Library, 1930.

Migne, Jacques-Paul, ed. *Patrologiæ cursus completus Series græca.* 161 vols. Paris: Migne, 1857-1866.

_____. *Patrologiæ cursus completus…Series Latina.* 221 vols. Paris: Migne, 1844-1879.

The Passing of Mary: First Latin Form in *The Twelve Patriarchs, Excerpts and Epistles, The Clementina, Apocrypha, Decretals, Memoirs of Edessa and Syriac Documents, Remains of the First Ages.* Vol. 8 of *Ante-Nicene Fathers.* Edited by Alexander Roberts and James Donaldson. New York: The Christian Literature Company, 1890-1897, 592-94.

The Passing of Mary: Second Latin Form in *The Twelve Patriarchs, Excerpts and Epistles, The Clementina, Apocrypha, Decretals, Memoirs of Edessa and Syriac Documents, Remains of the First Ages.* Vol. 8 of *Ante-Nicene Fathers.* Edited by Alexander Roberts and James Donaldson. New York: The Christian Literature Company, 1890-1897, 595-98.

Peter Chrysologus, Saint. *Saint Peter Chrysologus: Selected Sermons; and Saint Valerian: Homilies.* Translated by George E. Ganss. New York: Fathers of the Church, Inc., 1953.

_____. *St. Peter Chrysologus: Selected Sermons*. Vol. 2. Translated by William B. Palardy. Washington, DC: Catholic University of America Press, 2004.

The Philokalia: The Complete Text; Compiled by St. Nikodemus of the Holy Mountain and St. Makarius of Corinth. Translated and edited by G.E.H. Palmer, Philip Sherrard, and Kallistos Ware. 4 vols. London: Faber and Faber Limited, 1979-1995.

The Qu'ran. Translated by E.H. Palmer. Oxford: The Clarendon Press, 1900.

Theodore of Studites, Saint. *St. Theodore of Studites on the Holy Icons*. Translated by Catharine Roth. Crestwood: St. Vladimir's Seminary Press, 1981.

Theodosius of Alexandria, Saint. *The Falling Asleep of Mary* in *Coptic Apocryphal Gospels: Translations Together with the Texts of Some of Them*. Translated by Forbes Robinson. Cambridge: University Press, 1896, 90-127.

SECONDARY SOURCES

Allchin, A.M. *Wholeness and Transfiguration: Illustrated in the Lives of St. Francis of Assisi and St. Seraphim of Sarov*. Fairacres, Oxford: SLG Press, The Convent of the Incarnation, 1974.

Baggley, John. *Doors of Perception: Icons and their Spiritual Significance*. London: Mowbray, 1987.

Beausobre, Julia de. *Flame in the Snow: A Life of St. Seraphim of Sarov*. Springfield: Templegate Publishers, 1996.

Billington, James H. *The Icon and the Axe: An Interpretive History of Russian Culture*. New York: Knopf, 1966.

Boosalis, Harry M. *Joy of the Holy: St. Seraphim of Sarov and Orthodox Spiritual Life*. South Canaan: St. Tikhon's Seminary Press, 1993.

Bryer, Anthony and Mary Cunningham, eds. *Mount Athos and Byzantine Monasticism: Papers from the Twenty-eighth*

Spring Symposium of Byzantine Studies, Birmingham, March 1994. Brookfield, VT: Variorum, 1996.

Bulgakov, Sergius. *A Bulgakov Anthology.* Edited by James Pain and Nicolas Zernov. Philadelphia: Westminster Press, 1976.

_____. *The Orthodox Church.* Rev. ed. Crestwood: St. Vladimir's Seminary Press, 1988.

Buursma, Bruce. "Greek Orthodox Leader Calls Weeping Madonna Icon a Sign, not a Miracle." *Chicago Tribune.* February 11, 1987, 3.

Byron, Robert. *The Station Athos: Treasures and Men.* London: Duckworth, 1928.

Cauvin, Henri E. "Believers Still Flock to Cicero Icon." *Chicago Tribune.* July 15, 1994, 8.

Cavarnos, Constantine. *The Icon: Its Spiritual Basis and Purpose.* Belmont: Institute for Byzantine and Modern Greek Studies, 1973.

_____. *St. Arsenios of Paros: Remarkable Confessor, Spiritual Guide, Educator, Ascetic, Miracle-worker, and Healer; An Account of His Life, Character, Message and Miracles.* Belmont: Institute for Byzantine and Modern Greek Studies, 1978.

_____. *St. Cosmas Aitolos: Great Missionary, Awakener, Illuminator, and Holy Martyr of Greece: An Account of His Life, Character and Message, Including His Teaching on God, Heaven, and Hell, and His Prophecies, Together with Selections from His Sermons.* Belmont: Institute for Byzantine and Modern Greek Studies, 1985.

_____. *St. Macarios of Corinth: Archbishop of Corinth, Guardian of Sacred Tradition, Reviver of Orthodox Mysticism, Compiler of the Philokalia, Spiritual Striver, Enlightener and Guide, and Trainer of Martyrs: An Account of His Life, Character, and Message, Together with Selections from Three of His Publications.* Belmont: Institute for Byzantine and Modern Greek Studies, 1972.

_____. *St. Methodia of Kimolos: Remarkable Ascetic, Teacher of Virtue, Counselor, Comforter, and Healer(1865-1908): An Account of Her Life, Character, Miracles, and Influence, Together with Selected Hymns from the Akolouthia in Honor of Her, and a Letter to Her Sister Anna.* Belmont: Institute for Byzantine and Modern Greek Studies, 1987.

_____. *St. Nicodemos the Hagiorite: Great Theologian and Teacher of the Orthodox Church, Reviver of Hesychasm, Moralist, Canonist, Hagiologist, and Writer of Liturgical Poetry: An Account of His Life, Character and Message, Together with a Comprehensive List of His Writings and Selections from Them.* Belmont: Institute for Byzantine and Modern Greek Studies, 1974.

_____. *St. Nikephoros of Chios: Outstanding Writer of Liturgical Poetry and Lives of Saints, Educator, Spiritual Striver, and Trainer of Martyrs: An Account of His Life, Character and Message, Together with a Comprehensive List of His Publications, Selections from Them, and Brief Biographies of Eleven Neomartyrs and Other Orthodox Saints Who are Treated in His Works.* Belmont: Institute for Byzantine and Modern Greek Studies, 1976.

_____. *Saints Raphael, Nicholas and Irene of Lesvos.* Belmont: Institute for Byzantine and Modern Greek Studies, 1990.

Clendenin, Daniel B. *Eastern Orthodox Christianity: A Western Perspective.* 2nd ed. Grand Rapids: Baker Academic, 2005.

_____. *Eastern Orthodox Theology: A Contemporary Reader.* 2nd ed. Grand Rapids: Baker Academic, 2004.

Connor, Carolyn L. *Art and Miracles in Medieval Byzantium: The Crypt at Hosios Loukas and Its Frescoes.* Princeton: Princeton University Press, 1991.

"Cyprus Icon is Said to Weep." *New York Times.* February 10, 1997.

Dawkins, Richard McGillivray. *The Monks of Mount Athos.* London: G. Allen & Unwin, Ltd, 1936.

Doulis, Thomas, ed. *Journeys to Orthodoxy: A Collection of Essays by Converts to Orthodox Christianity.* Minneapolis: Light and Life, 1986.

Evdokimov, Paul. *The Art of the Icon: A Theology of Beauty.* Torrance: Oakwood, 1990 [*Art de l'icône; théologie de la beauté.* Paris: Desclée De Brouwer, 1972].

_____. *St. Seraphim of Sarov: An Icon of Orthodox Spirituality.* Minneapolis: Light and Life Publishing Company, Inc., 1988.

Fedotov, Georgy Petrovich, ed. *A Treasury of Russian Spirituality.* Mineola: Dover Publications, Inc., 2003.

_____. *A Treasury of Russian Spirituality.* http://www/holytrinitymission.org/books/english/russian_spirituality_fedotov.htm (March 4, 2008).

Freely, John. *The Cyclades: Discovering the Greek Islands of the Aegean.* London: I.B. Tauris, 2006.

Frisch, Suzy. "Virgin Mary Apparition on Window Draws Faithful." *Chicago Tribune.* May 22, 1997, 1.

Galloway, Paul. "And Now, the Tears Flow Again; Church Takes Low-key Tack with Icon's Latest Weeping." *Chicago Tribune.* July 26, 1995, 1.

"Glorification of the Venerable Herman of Alaska, Wonderworker of All America." http://www.ocafs.oca.org/FeastSaintsLife.asp?FSID=102241 (March 18, 2008).

Golder, Frank Alfred. *Father Herman, Alaska's Saint; A Preliminary Account of the Life and Miracles of Blessed Father Herman.* Willits: Eastern Orthodox Books, 1972.

"The Guiding Mother of God Weeping Icon." http://www.visionsofjesuschrist. com/weeping48.htm (October 12, 2007).

Gorainoff, Irina. *Séraphim de Sarov.* Bégrolles-en-Mauges: Abbaye de Bellefontaine, 1973.

Gross, Tom. "Are Tears Flowing from Jesus Painting?" *Jerusalem Post Service*, December 6, 1996.

_____. "Miracle Declared in Bethlehem as Jesus Weeps." *Jerusalem Post*, November 28, 1996.

Hadjicostis, Menelaos. "Weeping Icon Moves a Nation." *Cyprus News Agency*. February 7, 1997.

Hasluck, Frederick Willliam. *Athos and its Monasteries*. London: K. Paul, Trench, Trubner & Co. Ltd, 1924.

Hellier, Chris. *Monasteries of Greece*. London: Tauris Parke, 1996.

Hirsley, Michael. "Icon's Tears are Turning into a Stream of People." *Chicago Tribune*. May 6, 1994, 1.

The Holy and Great Monastery of Vatopaidi: Tradition, History, Art. Mount Athos: The Monastery, 1998.

Johnston, William M., ed., *Encyclopedia of Monastaicism*. 2 vols. Chicago: Fitzroy Dearborn, 2000.

Kadas, Sotiris. *Mount Athos: An Illustrated Guide to the Monasteries and their History*. Athens: Ekdotike Athenon, 1980.

Kavvadias, Tasia. "Icon's Miraculous Sign Draws Multitude." *Chicago Tribune*. December 15, 1986, 1.

Kessel, Jerrold." "Jesus Painting Said to Wink and Shed Tears in Bethlehem," November 29, 1996. www.cnn.com/WORLD/9611/29/weeping.jesus/index.html (December 7, 2007).

Kolarz, Walter. *Religion in the Soviet Union*. New York: St. Martin's Press; London: MacMillan and Company, 1961.

Kologrivof, *Essai sur la sainteté en Russie*. Bruges: Beyaert, 1953.

Kontzevitch, Helen. *Saint Seraphim: Wonderworker of Sarov*. Translated by St. Xenia Skete. Wildwood: Saint Xenia Skete, 2004.

Lassus, Louis-Albert. *Staretz Séraphim de Sarov: joie et lumière*. Paris: O.E.I.L., 1984.

Laub, Karin. "Blinking Jesus Declared Miracle." *Times-Picayune*, November 29, 1996, A25.

Locin, Mitchell. "Icon's Tears Bring Smiles to Parishioners." *Chicago Tribune.* December 12, 1986, 1.

_____. "Visitors to Icon Force Church to Cut its Hours." *Chicago Tribune.* January 14, 1987, 8.

_____. "Weeping Icon Draws Worshipers." *Chicago Tribune*, December 9, 1986, 3.

Lossky, Vladimir. *The Mystical Theology of the Eastern Church.* Translated by members of the Fellowship of St. Albans and St. Sergius. London: J. Clarke, 1957 [*Essai sur la théologie mystique de l'Eglise d'Orient.* Paris: Aubier, 1944].

Merrill, Christopher. *Things of the Hidden God: Journey to the Holy Mountain.* New York: Random House, 2005.

Mileant, Bishop Alexander, ed. "Saint Herman of Alaska." http://www.fatheralexander.org/ booklets/english/herman.htm (March 18, 2008).

_____. "Saint Seraphim of Sarov: On Acquisition of the Holy Spirit." http://www. fatheralexander.org/booklets/ english/sermon_st_seraphim.htm (February 29, 2008).

_____. "St. Seraphim of Sarov: Life and Teachings." Translated by Nicholas and Natalia Semyanko. http://www/fatheralexander.org/booklets/english/seraphim_e.htm (February 29, 2008).

Nightingale, Benedict. "Greek Islands to Call Home." *New York Times*, September 28, 1997.

Norwich, John Julius and Reresby Sitwell. *Mount Athos.* London: Hutchinson, 1966.

Oikonomake-Papadopoulou, Giota. *Enkolpia: The Holy and Great Monastery of Vatopaidi.* Mount Athos: The Holy and Great Monastery of Vatopaidi, 2001.

Ouspensky, Leonid. *Theology of the Icon.* Translated by Anthony Gythiel with selections translated by Elizabeth Meyendorff. 2 vols. Crestwood: St. Vladimir's Seminary Press, 1992 [*Théologie de l'icône dans l'Eglise orthodoxe.* Paris: Editions du Cerf, 1980].

Ouspensky, Leonid and Vladimir Lossky. *The Meaning of Icons.* Translated by G.E.H. Palmer and E. Kadloubovsky. Rev. ed. Crestwood: St. Vladimir's Seminary Press, 1982.

Papadopoulos, Stelios. *The Holy Xenophontos Monastery: The Icons.* Mount Athos: the Holy Xenophontos Monastery, 1999.

_____., ed. *Simonopetra, Mount Athos.* Athens: ETBA, Hellenic Industrial Development Bank SA, 1991.

Papadopoulos, Stelios and Chrysoula Kapioldassi-Soteropoulou, eds. *Icons of the Holy Monastery of Pantokrator.* Mount Athos: Pantokrator Holy Monastery, 1998.

Pelikan, Jaroslav. *Imago Dei: The Byzantine Apologia for Icons.* Washington, DC: National Gallery of Art; Princeton: Princeton University Press, 1990.

Pius XII, Pope. *Munificentissimus Deus.* http://www.ewtn.com/ library/PAPALDOC/ P12MUNIF. HTM (November 2, 2007).

Pospielovsky, Dimitry. *The Russian Church under the Soviet Regime 1917-1982.* 2 vols. Crestwood: St. Vladimir's Seminary Press, 1984.

Quenot, Michel. *Du Dieu-homme à l'homme-dieu: l'image de la sainteté et la sainteté des images.* Paris. Cerf, 2004.

_____. *The Icon: Window on the Kingdom.* Translated by a Carthusian monk. Crestwood: St. Vladimir's Seminary Press, 1991 [*L'icône: Fenêtre sur l'absolu.* Paris: Cerf, 1987].

_____. *The Resurrection and the Icon.* Crestwood: St. Vladimir's Seminary Press, 1997 [*La Résurrection et l'icône.* Paris: Editions Mame, 1992].

Roberts, Penny. "Many Find Miracle in Weeping Mary." *Chicago Tribune.* April 25, 1994, 3.

Rochcau, Vsévolod. *Saint Séraphim, Sarov et Divéyevo: études et documents: suivis d'une étude sur un fragment inédit des Récits d'un pèlerin russe.* Bégrolles-en-Mauges: Abbaye de Bellefontaine, 1987.

Rose, Father Seraphim, and Abbot Herman Podmoshensky. *Northern Thebaid: Monastic Saints of the Russian North.* Platina: Saint Herman Press, 1995.

Sahas, Daniel J. *Icon and Logos: Sources in Eighth-Century Iconoclasm.* Toronto: University of Toronto Press, 1986.

Sarlas, Elaine. "Weeping Icon." *Chicago Tribune.* January 27, 1987, 10.

Schmemann, Serge. "Arafat Speaks to Throngs in Bethlehem." *New York Times,* December 24, 1995, 1.9.

_____. "Arafat Visits Liberated Bethlehem." *Times-Picayune,* December 24, 1995, A.3.

_____. "In the Land of Faith, a Time for Utter Disbelief." *New York Times,* March 10, 2002, 4.1.

Seigel, Jessica. "Faithful Gather to See Icon's Tears." *Chicago Tribune.* September 11, 1988, 3.

Sendler, Egon. *The Icon, Image of the Invisible: Elements of Theology, Aesthetics and Technique.* Translated by Fr. Steven Bigham. Redondo Beach: Oakwood Publications, 1988 [*L'Icône, image de l'invisible: Eléments de théologie, esthétique et technique.* Paris: Desclée De Brouwer, 1981.

Sherrard, Philip. *Athos: The Holy Mountain.* Photographs by Takis Zervoulakos. London: Sidgwick & Jackson, 1982.

_____. *Athos, the Mountain of Silence.* London: Oxford University Press, 1960.

_____. *The Sacred in Life and Art.* Ipswich: Golgonooza Press, 1990.

Shevzov, Vera. *Russian Orthodoxy on the Eve of Revolution.* New York: Oxford University Press, 2004.

Smith, Wes. "Icon, Air Controller Get Credit in Miracle." *Chicago Tribune.* December 31, 1986, 1.

Speake, Graham. *Mount Athos: Renewal in Paradise.* New Haven: Yale University Press, 2002.

Stamoolis, James J. *Eastern Orthodox Mission Theology Today.* Maryknoll: Orbis Books, 1986.

Struve, Nikita A. *Christians in Contemporary Russia*. Translated by Lancelot Sheppard and A. Manson. London: Harvill, 1967.

Theocharides, Ploutarchos, Pandelis Foundas, and Stergios Stefanou. *Mount Athos*. Translated by Philip Ramp. Athens: Melissa Publishing House, 1992.

"Throngs Flock to Weeping Virgin." *San Francisco Chronicle*. December 23, 1986, 12.

Trubetskoi, Eugene N. *Icons: Theology in Color*. Translated by Gertrude Vakar. Introduction by George M.A. Hanfmann. Crestwood: St. Vladimir's Seminary Press, 1973.

Ugolnik, Anthony. *The Illuminating Icon*. Grand Rapids: Eerdmans, 1988.

Walter, Christopher. *Art and Ritual of the Byzantine Church*. Preface by Robin Cormack. London: Variorum, 1982.

_____. *Iconography of Constantine the Great, Emperor and Saint with Associated Studies*. Leiden: Alexandros Press, 2006.

_____. *Studies in Byzantine Iconography*. London: Variorum Reprints, 1977.

_____. *The Warrior Saints in Byzantine Art and Tradition*. Aldershot: Ashgate, 2003.

Ware, Kallistos, Bishop. *The Orthodox Way*. Crestwood: St. Vladimir's Seminary Press, 1995.

Ware, Timothy. *The Orthodox Church*. Rev. ed. London: Penguin Books, 1997.

"Weeping Icon Called Miraculous Sign." *Los Angeles Times*. January 3, 1987, 13.

"Weeping Icon Stops its Crying." *Chicago Tribune*. July 18, 1987, 5.

"Weeping Icon Watched." *Houston Chronicle*. December 12, 1986, 10.

"Weeping Virgin Icon Draws Throngs to Chicago." *New York Times*. December 22, 1986, B16.

Williamson, Elizabeth. "Russian Faithful Turn to Mummy at a Time of Great Stress, Discovery of a Monk's Suspected Remains Has Been Proclaimed a Miracle." *Chicago Tribune*. January 3, 1999, 5.

Zander, Valerie. *St. Seraphim of Sarov*. Translated by Sister Gabriel Anne and introduced by Father Boris Bobrinskoy. London: The Society for Promoting Christian Knowledge, 1975.

Zorn, Eric. "Icon Is Still Crying for our Attention." *Chicago Tribune*. May 15, 1994, 1.

D

E

F

G

H

I

J